REDNECKS
and other
BONAFIDE
AMERICANS

REDNECKS and other BONAFIDE AMERICANS

Bo Whaley

<small>SECOND EDITION</small>

RUTLEDGE HILL PRESS
Nashville, Tennessee

Other books by the author:

Gunracks & Six Packs
A Redneck Bites the Big Apple
Kudzu Don't Cover Everything
Why The South Lost the War
All I Ever Wanted Was a Piece of Cornbread and a Cadillac
Bo Whaley's Field Guide to Southern Women
How to Love Yankees with a Clear Conscience
The Official Redneck Handbook
Redneckin' Made Easy

Copyright © 1986, 1991 Bo Whaley

Published in Nashville, Tennessee, by Rutledge Hill Press, Inc.
211 Seventh Avenue North, Nashville, Tennessee 37219

Typography by ProtoType Graphics, Inc. and Bailey Typography

Library of Congress Cataloging-in-Publication Data

Whaley, Bo, 1926 —
    Rednecks and other bonafide Americans / Bo Whaley. — 2nd ed.
        p.   cm.
    ISBN 1-55853-106-8
    1. United States — Social life and customs — 1971-   — Humor.
    2. Whaley, Bo, 1926 —   — Humor.   I. Title
    E169.04.W48   1991
    973.92 — dc20   91-10858
                                                                          CIP

3 4 5 6 7 8 — 99 98 97
Manufactured in the United States of America

Dedication

To Jimmy Cook, who has more guts than a
    fiddle factory;
more nerve than a broken tooth;
more courage than a commando;
more patience than a fisherman;
and more determination than a beginning
    skater.
And faith.
He has the "Faith of Our Fathers."
He's my friend.

Contents

REDNECKS
and other
BONAFIDE
AMERICANS

Part 1

Rednecks . . .
They Really Are For Real

What, exactly, is a redneck? This is a question that has cried out for an answer ever since Adam popped the first wad of Levi Garrett in his mouth and Eve cautioned him not to spit on the astro-turf.

Here, then, are the conclusions of one redneck researcher who has considered the question for more than forty years.

A redneck is a mysterious sort of character who drives a four-wheel drive pickup with oversize tires on the first floor and a cab perched on the eighth, flanked by twin CB antennas, with a fish stringer hanging from the inside rear-view mirror. He's a shaggy-haired varmint who hasn't seen a barber since Sal Maglie retired from baseball, sports a beard, and wears a Cat Diesel cap, black with yellow patch. In his left shirt pocket is a barely visible pouch of Levi Garrett chewing tobacco, with an equally subdued pack of Winstons in his right. A 30-06 rifle (with scope) and a .12 gauge Remington Model 1100 shotgun, along with a reel and rod, hang in the back window above the decal of a Confederate flag that bears the reminder: Hell No! I Ain't Forgettin! And there are three bumper stickers: How 'Bout Them Dawgs?!, Get Your Heart in America or Get Your (picture of a donkey) Out!, and next to it is one with a forefinger pointed skyward that says I Found It!

Those are the back bumper. On the front under the grille is a personalized tag that reads, Joe Boy and Willie Kate.

He's driving with a long-neck Bud in one hand, a large portion of Willie Kate in the other, and they listen as Waylon and Willie and the boys knock out their theme song, "Luckenbach Texas," on the AM-FM stereo tape player.

And, they're headed to . . . wherever, to do . . . whatever.

Redneck Research Can Be Hazardous

WITH COMPLETE DISREGARD for my own safety, I've gone to great lengths to gather data regarding the stereotyped redneck. Throwing caution and good judgment to the wind, I invaded beer joints, all-night coffee houses, VFW dances, juke joints, and wrestling matches from Dry Branch to Donalsonville. I still don't have the answer to my question, "What is a redneck?"

Some replies are printable; some not. Here are a few that are:

"A guy with a chip on his shoulder lookin' for somebody to knock it off."

"Trouble-maker. A born troublemaker. That's what a redneck is."

"A rebel. Anti-everything. Lives off beer, cigarettes, and beef jerky."

"A know-it-all who don't know nothin'."

"He's stupid. People laugh at him but he ain't got the sense to know it."

"Thinks he's a real ladies' man. Hah! Couldn't get a date in a women's prison."

There's more to this research business than meets the eye.

I walked into a cafe next to a pool room down near the Florida line. The front door screen was torn and a lug wrench was on the pinball machine next to a tattered copy of *Parts Pups*. What really caught my eye was the sign above the grill: "Notice—We Don't Cook No Omlits."

Next, I had a memorable experience in a quaint little establishment between West Green and Broxton. Not only did I inquire about rednecks there, I wound up face to face with one—and he did all the questioning.

I played it straight, asking the waitress my well-worn question, "In your opinion, what is a redneck?"

"A redneck? There's one right over there in that booth by the juke box. Hey, Buster! Drag it over here and talk to this here newspaper man," she shouted.

Caught! I was caught in a REDSCAM of my own design. I'd have been glad to buy Buster an omlit and vamoose. Ever seen an elephant get up? Lord, I thought Buster never was gonna get through gettin' up. He finally made it and ambled over to the counter where I stood—trembling.

"Yeah, what is it, Hoss?" he grunted, settling his 6'6"-280-pound frame on the next stool.

I didn't get to answer. Miss Big Mouth did it for me. "Man's wantin' to learn somethin' 'bout rednecks. He's from the newspaper," she blurted out before I had a chance to lie or run.

"Newspaper man? Where 'bouts you from, Cuz, Atlanter?" he asked through his beard and kitchen match.

"No, sir, but I'll move there if you want me to. I'm from Dublin," I stammered.

I explained my mission and, thank God, he understood. Actually, I was all set to go flyin' over the counter to join the dirty dishes and cold French fries. My epitaph flashed before my eyes: "Bo Whaley. Died March 28, 1981, Between the Dirty Dishes and Cold French Fries, From Multiple Head Wounds in Leona's Lunch."

"Really, I don't know what a redneck is. I'm just trying to . . ."

"Well, put this down in your little book, Cuz. Damn right I'm a redneck. Don't take nothin' off nobody. I drink Blue Ribbon beer, been married twice and was drunk both times. Shacked up more times than I can remember and got little Busters strewed from here to Nashville, and I ain't through yet. I'm thirty-seven years old, a veteran, and don't hit a lick at a snake 'less I have to. Chew Levi Garrett and ain't got no use for them B—'s in Washington, and Atlanter ain't no better. Live in a trailer, by myself most of the time, down by the river. I got a '68 pickup and listen to Willie Nelson, Moe and Joe, and Loretter Lynn. Ain't had a tie on since grandpa's funeral in '63. I like my eggs fried hard and can't remember a week when I ain't got drunk. Fact is, I'm runnin' late, Cuz. Anything else you wanna' know?"

"No, sir, Mr. Buster. That's fine, sir, just fine. Thank you, sir," I said, humbly.

He spanked Leona on the rear and ambled out the front door. A redneck? I have to think so. A thoroughbred.

Like I said in the beginning, "with complete disregard for my own safety . . . ."

I was eating breakfast in a place near Darien. I had the guy at the next table pegged as a redneck. His table manners were awful. He slurped his coffee, propped his feet on a chair, and ate his sausage with his hands. When he finished he struck a stick match with his thumbnail and lit a Camel. Filter? Perish the thought.

He and the waitress were obviously at odds. I heard her mutter something about, "the night you whupped up on Ralph," before taking a swing at him with a butcher knife. Such upbringing! When she swung the butcher knife, I dang near dropped a whole handful of grits!

Know Where Redneck Hunters Look?

Take it from me, you gotta' go south to find pedigreed rednecks, the real thoroughbreds.

The best place to find them is in juke joints, and notice I didn't say night clubs, supper clubs, cabarets, or social halls. Rednecks come to roost in juke joints Friday and Saturday nights. Now then, when I say juke joint, I mean a down-yonder, roll-up-your-sleeves, bring-me-another-beer, every-man (and woman)-for-himself, three bucks to get in and $37.85 to get out, Willie Nelson-Conway Twitty-Loretta Lynn establishment where they stamp your hand when you spring for the three and suck up your $37.85 like an Electrolux. That, good buddy, is where you find the thoroughbreds.

I went south on my motorcycle. Credentials, man; you gotta' have 'em. I wouldn't leave home without 'em on a juke joint excursion.

I found a redneck roost near the Altamaha River. The sign said, "Daisy Mae's Place—Cold Beer and Fish Baits." I parked between a four-wheel-drive Blazer and a Jeep featuring pink carpet. Are you with me? The bumper sticker on the Jeep suggested a solution to a Sunday morning problem: Sure Cure for Hangovers—Don't Sober Up.

The clock on the Blue Ribbon sign indicated it was 8:40 P.M. as I dropped three ones on the table at the door and had my hand stamped.

"Been here before, buddy?" she asked.

"No ma'am, first time," I replied.

"O.K. The stamp means you can go outside and to the men's room as many times as you want to. Just stick it under the light when you come back in."

"My hand?"

"Right. You got it, good buddy. Next? That'll be three dollars. You been here . . . ?"

Properly branded, I felt my way into the main arena and sat at a table near the bandstand, but not for long because this girl waitress wearing either very short shorts or a wide belt suddenly appeared.

"Can't sit here, mister. This is Rooster's table," she said.

"Oh? Who's Rooster?"

"Never mind. Rooster just don't like nobody settin' at his table 'less he asks 'em."

Know what I did? I moved to another table. I didn't pass Good Judgment 101 at Georgia Southern by taking foolish chances. After all, a table is a table, right?

I sat and waited, eyeing Rooster's table. I wanted to see that cat. At 8:55 by the Blue Ribbon clock he strolled in, walked right by the handstamper like she wasn't there, slowing down just long enough to sling a little currency her way. Hand stamp? Forget it! When Rooster wants to go to the men's room he don't need no hand stamp to get back inside.

Rooster walked straight to "his" table, but didn't sit down. He never sat down all night, just propped his cowboy-boot-clad foot in the chair and leaned on the back of it. He could have had a spot on the bandstand. Rooster is definitely the "cock of the walk" at Daisy Mae's.

When Rooster Roberts walks in a juke joint, everybody who is able stands up and takes notice. Those unable to stand simply wave as he strolls by. You can't miss him. He wears Western shirts, Levis held up by a belt with a buckle only slightly smaller than a sheet of plywood, and Western boots with toes sharp-pointed enough to thread a needle with. Rooster's real trademark, though, is the ever-present stick match in his mouth.

"Ain't never seen Rooster without his match," Rita, the waitress allowed. "Stays right there whenever he eats, drinks, smokes, dances, or, uh, whatever."

I knew I had to try it even if I got my head knocked off, so I walked over to Rooster's table and asked him, "Excuse me, sir, but do you have a match?"

"Nope, not since Superman died," he replied. Of course, I could have asked for the one stuck in his mouth, but would have had more success attempting to extract his wisdom teeth.

"Pretty slim pickins tonight, Hoss," he said.

"How's that?" I asked.

"Gals. Nothin' much worth lookin' at 'cept maybe that'n over there by the juke box. Hey, Rita!" he yelled.

"Yeah, whatcha' want, Rooster, a beer?"

"Naw, give that ol' gal over there by the juke one an' tell her I bought it," he ordered. Then, turning back to me he said, "Set y'sef down if y'want to."

I pulled up a chair, propped my foot in it and watched Rita deliver the beer and the message to "that ol' gal" who, by my arithmetic, measured in the neighborhood of 37-22-36, and that ain't a bad neighborhood. Once, when she stood to adjust whatever women stand up to adjust, I had to change my calculations because if those jeans with the little pony on the back pocket ever busted, the measurements would change to 37-22 and a bunch. Swift never packed a tighter package.

Rooster sent a steady stream of Blue Ribbons to "that ol' gal" and finally made his move shortly after midnight when he called for Rita, peeled a ten-spot off a roll, and said, "Tell them jokers to play my song." Rita was well-schooled and shortly them jokers played "For the Good Times," and Rooster danced with "that ol' gal." The jeans held, thank God.

When the song ended, Rooster returned to his table and propped.

"You really like that song, huh?" I asked.

"Only one I dance to, Hoss. You can have that fast mess. I ain't dancin' with no gal I can't squeeze."

That, friends and neighbors, is Rooster Roberts, cock of the walk at "Daisy Mae's Place—Cold Beer and Fish Baits."

Country songs are mostly sad songs with such tear-jerking lines as "Three hungry children and a crop in the field; you picked a fine time to leave me, Lucille," "Ruby, don't take your love to town," "When your girlfriend writes a letter to your wife." Sad words, sure, but not nearly as sad as those sung to Rooster by "that ol' gal."

She was busy collecting her Salem 100s and Bic lighter and stuffing her shoulder bag when Rooster hit her with, "Come on, baby. Let's go to my place down on the river."

"Can't. Goin' to S'vanner with the guitar picker," she said. The saddest lyrics ever written? You better believe it. After Rooster invested twelve dollars in beer and the guitar picker hadn't even bought her a Slim Jim, she comes up with, "I'm goin' with the guitar picker."

Rooster watched him put his Fender electric in the case, grab what was left of the last Blue Ribbon Rita had delivered to "that ol' gal," and leave with her. Rooster couldn't believe it.

"Damn, Rita! He looks like a commercial for embalming fluid. What's he got that I ain't got?" Rooster asked.

"I can tell you but you won't like it, Rooster."

"Go ahead!"

"A Fender electric guitar that he knows how to pick, 'that ol' gal' you been buyin' beer for all night, and what's left of the last Blue Ribbon you bought her."

"Yeah, guess you're right. I'll wait for you in the truck, Rita."

"Ten-four, Rooster."

I left and headed home, thinking about Rooster. Somebody ought to write a song about him. I hummed the lyrics, sad lyrics, as I tooled up U.S. 1 on my Harley: "Sorry, but I'm goin' with the guitar picker."

The Critters Just Ain't Understood

I've done a lot of research on the subject of rednecks and have reached some definite conclusions about the critters. There are some big misconceptions about them.

For instance, somewhere along the well-worn longneck Bud and Red Man trail, rednecks have been repeatedly characterized as male, bearded and profane. This just ain't true, Hoss. Some are female, bearded, and profane.

Another thing my research determined is the best time to go redneck hunting and where to find 'em.

Prime time is between 9:00 P.M. and 4:00 A.M. Where? Likely redneck roosts are juke joints and all-night cafes where a weary traveler can purchase "two aigs scrambled hard, with meat, grits, toast, and a Pepsi," along with $6.00 worth of Willie Nelson and $4.00 worth of Johnny Paycheck, unsolicited, for the bargain price of $1.85.

And if you look innocent enough, or dumb enough, and non-law-enforcement enough, you stand a good chance of participating in a "friendly" game of stud, draw, blackjack, knock, or gin—whether you want to or not.

I happened to be down in Liberty County not long ago. I might mention right here that unless you live there, work there, have been sent there, or took the wrong road and wound up there, the only real reason to be in Liberty County is to "happen to be there." Nobody I know goes there on purpose.

How do you go to Liberty County? Two ways, good buddy: infrequently and cautiously. (And, after writing this, not at all, for me.)

Having lived there once, I'm convinced that Liberty County has two prime industries, Fort Stewart and juke joints. The reason for the juke joints is Fort Stewart. What is a juke joint, you ask? Oh, you poor, sheltered soul. I'll tell you what; take four pieces of scrap plywood, six cases of longneck Bud, a neon sign, a jukebox filled with country and western records and you got yourself one.

Who goes to juke joints, you ask? You guessed it, Clyde—rednecks. And another thing; you can open up a juke joint and put anything you like on the neon sign out front—Chez Liberty, Follies Hinesville, Mighty Midway, or Lucille's Place—it matters not to the rednecks who will frequent it. They're gonna' call it "The Juke," no matter what.

It's just a fact of life. You find rednecks in juke joints.

Oh, hold the phone! I left out one very important thing common to every juke joint, the pool table. You gotta' have a pool table. And if you're wise, you won't dare shoot eight-ball with Lucille.

From 1966 through 1973, I, along with many other FBI agents, had more than a passing interest in an establishment located on U.S. 17 near the Liberty-McIntosh County line, a truck stop—an unusual truck stop.

It's the only truck stop I've ever seen that had no gas pumps. Oil? Not a drop on the premises. Jukebox? Yeah. Longneck Bud?

Yes. Red Man? Yeah. Stud, draw, blackjack, knock, or gin? Yeah. Plus country and western twenty-four hours a day.

Entertainment? You better believe it. It wasn't unusual back in the late 60s to observe as many as a dozen eighteen-wheelers lined up out front on U.S. 17.

The ol' truck stop may have been the only one in the good ol' U.S. of A. where you had to be a member to get in to find out what went on "Behind the Green Door."

And one of the feature attractions was Robbie Nell Bell, known to one and all in that area as "Robbie Nail Bail, fum Almer," a real downyonder redneck, a sight to behold and a joy to just hold.

Robbie Nail Is Top Choice for Redneck of Year

I just introduced you to Robbie Nell Bell, "fum Almer."

Let me set the record straight here and now about Robbie Nell. Oh, that's her name all right. But that ain't what you hear when she says it.

It just sorta' comes out "Robbie Nail Bail," slow and easy like cane syrup in January. Robbie Nail also has two brothers, Fred and Jesse, whom she affectionately refers to as "Fray-ed" and "Jay-ssie." And she has an uncle in "Chicargo," and an "ain't on my mommer's side," in "Cissyrow, Illernoise."

I knew Robbie Nail was a winner when I saw her take off her United States Army field jacket, monogrammed, "Fincher— Second Battalion—Company C," and "thow it on a cheer over yonder by the winder," in Mel's Juke, about a six-pack north of Broxton.

Robbie Nail is a redneck and I couldn't have found a better one in the back of a four-wheel-drive pickup, in front of the cotton candy booth at the county fair, or at any tractor pull south of Dillon, South Carolina. She's my top choice for Redneck of the Year.

I sat and watched her awhile from my vantage point at the counter. Robbie Nail and her crew, Hawkeye, Big'un, Little Bit, Snake, and Ramrod, had staked their nightly claim on the back booth.

The jukebox wailed on and on, and loud, to the strains of some guy with a double hernia and a guitar coming on with "Daddy Died and Mama Cried, 'Cause His Insurance Had Done Lapsed."

Robbie Nail divided her time between lighting Salem 100s and coughing. Her long, straight hair (blonde this night but destined to change colors more times than a chameleon) kept getting in her beer. But she was in charge, the boss of the back booth.

"Put a quarter in the juke," she said to Hawkeye.

"Ain't got no quarter," he growled.

"What? You ain't even got a quarter and you talkin' 'bout takin' me to 'Jaykull?'" she barked.

Hawkeye remained silent and sulked.

I figured this was as good a time as any to make my entrance so I reached for a quarter.

"What y'all wanna' hear?" I asked of the back booth, of no one in particular.

"J-7," replied Robbie Nail, answering for everybody. Like I said, she was in charge of the back booth.

I dropped my quarter in and punched J-7, thereby bringing Willie Nelson to center stage to sing "On the Road Again."

"Got one more," I said. "What'll it be?"

"Punch it again," Robbie Nail said.

"What? J-7?"

"That's a big Ten-four, Charlie," she said.

I did as requested and started to move back to the counter when I heard Robbie Nail say, "C'mon back and set with us if y'wanna', we ain't paticlar."

"Shoot naw! I even set with a Yankee once't," Snake said.

"I betcha' yore daddy didn' know 'bout it," said Big'un.

"Ya' better b'lieve he didn'," Snake said.

Little Bit came to life just long enough to bum a Salem from Robbie Nail and make her contribution to the conversation. "Where 'bouts was he from?"

"Damfino. N'oth Caliner, Kentucky—one o' them No'then states," Snake recalled.

Meanwhile, Mel had sauntered back to try and make a nickel. "What'll you have?"

"Lowenbrau," I said matter-of-factly.

"Don't sell no wine in here. Just beer," Mel said just as matter-of-factly.

I settled for a Miller Lite and gave it to Robbie Nail and Little Bit.

The conversation ranged from Reagan to J.B. Stoner, Hosea Williams to Culver Kidd. Kidd always did keep good company.

"Where 'bouts you from?" asked Robbie Nail.

"Dublin. Ever been there?"

"Reckon not. Mommer don't 'low me to go out of the state," she said.

I didn't pursue that.

"I seen ya' reading th' paper up at th' counter," said Little Bit. "What's th' news?"

"Oh, I was just reading about a guy in New York who was convicted for raping a nun, stabbing a priest, and stealing all the money from a Catholic church," I said.

"Damn, tha's downright terribl'," said Little Bit. "What'd they giv' 'im?"

"Hmmmmmm, let's see," I said, as I reached back for the paper. "Yeah, here it is. He got a total of 730 years."

"The SOB, they orta' giv' 'im life," growled Robbie Nail.

Robbie Nail Can Handle Them Yankees

Robbie Nail, "fum Almer," is as real as streak-o-lean, salt mackerel, and chitlins.

A real down-home American, she demands little except to be left alone to "do her thing," when she pleases, where she pleases, and with whom she pleases. And, she'll cut you if you run down America, mess with her man, or say bad things 'bout her "mommer."

She lives for country music, Salem Light 100s, Budweiser, and "my two young'uns, who live with my mommer."

Robbie Nail's ol' man is "somewhere in Tennysee and ain't sent a support check since just 'fore Thanksgiving 1979." She drives a 1973 Ford with a busted water pump and no spare tire and can pour cane syrup on a pair of cathead biscuits and never spill a drop.

Does she work? You better believe it, Hoss. She's the head waitress and music lover in charge of the jukebox at Mel's Juke and Bobby-Q, about a six-pack north of Broxton, and feeds quarters to the jukebox like a trained seal handler hands out dead fish.

Robbie Nail reads such classics as *True Confessions,* the *National Enquirer,* and anything written by Harold Robbins.

It was just over a year ago that Robbie Nail came face to face with a pair of New Jersey Americans in Mel's. She handled the encounter well.

The immigrants pulled up in front of Mel's and parked a big Cadillac between Ramrod's four-wheel-drive pickup and Hawkeye's Jeep. Naturally there were bags of Indian River grapefruit and oranges in the back seat, status symbols back in the Garden State that one has actually touched down on Florida soil.

The front bumper bore supporting evidence in the form of a Marineland sticker and the female of the pair sported a wrinkled suntan that all her friends at the deli in Jersey City would drool over.

The guy wore shorts and sandals and puffed on a big black cigar as long as a hoe handle that smelled like George Blackshear's cow lot on a rainy morning.

They selected a booth next to the very operative jukebox and the broken coat rack.

Robbie Nail closed in, leaned on the counter, and asked, "Y'all want bobby-q?"

"Do we have a choice?" asked the female New Jersey American.

"I reckon so. We got slyce't an' cheeupped."

"Is that all you'se got?" asked the male.

"Nope. We got pickled pigs feet and Slim Jims," she answered.

"Uggghh," grunted the female.

"Bring us two chipped with plenty of hot sauce," demanded the male.

"Anythin' to drink? We got Coke an' beer."

The male chose beer; the disappointed female selected Coke after determining there was no Tab.

In due time, after two heartbreaking selections on the jukebox, "I'm a Warm Hearted Man but Mama's Got Cold Feet" and "When Your Girlfriend Writes a Letter to Your Wife," Robbie Nail slid the bobby-q sandwiches, cheeupped, and the drinks in front of the furriners.

Within seconds, the male voiced another demand.

"Hey, girl! I specifically asked for hot sauce. Up where we

come from people know how to season food. Don't you have any hot barbecue sauce? This stuff is awful," he ranted.

She motioned for Mel to join her in the back.

"Ya' got any of y'r Aunt Minnie's hot pepper sauce left fum Christmas, Mel? Them Yankees out there in the front booth don't like y'r bobby-q sauce. The man says it ain't hot enough."

"Hmmmmm, lemme see. Last time I saw it I used it to start my outboard motor. It was right here by the kerosene and . . . oh yeah, here 'tis. But be careful," Mel cautioned.

After a generous dousing of both sandwiches with Aunt Minnie's special hot pepper sauce, Robbie Nail again slid them in front of the New Jersey Americans—and waited. But she didn't have to wait long.

"There, that's more like it," mumbled the male as he chomped on a large bite of his cheeupped and loaded bobby-q sandwich. "You just have to show these people down here in the South how to . . . Aaaahhhh! Wheeewww! I'm on fiiirrrre! Great God Almighty, my mouth is on fiiirrre! Water! Water! Bring me water, quick!"

Robbie Nail and Mel watched as he did an Indian fire dance past the juke, over a tackle box, and out the front door. His wife followed suit with her version of a New Jersey belly dancer before running into Hawkeye's Jeep.

When last seen, both were in the big ol' Cadillac, eating grapefruit and oranges by the dozen, and trying to get the car started.

"Yankee go home!" yelled Robbie Nail.

"And stay there!" echoed Mel.

Robbie Nail dropped a quarter in the juke, the cheeupped bobby-q sandwiches in the garbage can, and mumbled, "Mel, I jus' plain don't like no Yankees comin' down here an' tellin' me 'bout how t' fix bobby-q."

"Me neither, Robbie Nail. Now, how 'bout wipin' up that hot pepper sauce before it eats a hole in the counter," Mel said.

Is There No Culture in the South?

It happened to me again last week, at a cocktail party. I was backed into a corner by a pair of New Jersey American transplants, now enjoying the good life in Middle Georgia after serving a near-life sentence in the Garden State. I served a seven-year sentence there, myself, before being paroled to Georgia in August, 1965.

The whole thing started after I sat down at what I thought was an unoccupied table, bent on enjoying a cup of coffee. No way.

I had no more than sipped when they appeared at the table, took their seats, and introduced themselves. It seems that they were there before me but left to go wherever Yankee transplants go when they up and leave their table at a cocktail party.

Following the introductions, we engaged in the usual chatter that goes on at cocktail parties—the state of the weather, the state of the nation, high prices, the quality of the hors d'oeuvres, and family backgrounds—to establish the proper pedigree, you know.

I learned, among other things, that they migrated south from New Jersey after retirement. No surprise. I mean, after all, have you ever heard of anyone retiring to the North?

And they learned that I'd spent a few years in New Jersey, 1960-67, an eternity for a Georgia boy.

The conversation was rocking along smoothly until the female rubbed salt in my redneck wound with this observation: "I enjoy living down here in the South, except for one thing," she said, baiting me.

I took the bait and asked, "Yes? And what's that?"

"No culture. I miss the culture that I enjoyed in New Jersey and New York," she said.

I gritted my teeth real hard, gulped down what was left of my coffee, and counted to ten. I'd been in this corner before and really had no intention of making a scene. Finally, I asked her, "And what culture is it that you enjoyed up there that you miss so much down here?"

"Oh, things like the theater, art galleries, museums, excellent restaurants," she said. "Always something to do. But down here, nothing. Don't you find that to be true?"

"No, not really," I said. "It was my observation that of the eight million people in New York, about all 98 percent of them did was talk about the culture—the theatre, and such—but they never went."

"Well, at least it was there if you wanted it," she said.

I just had to ask the next question, and did.

"By the way, what prompted you two to move to Georgia? Do you have relatives here?"

"Oh, no. I just told Frank that the day he retired from his job in Brooklyn we were moving south, to either Florida or Georgia," she said. "We looked at Florida and decided on Georgia, Middle Georgia."

"A wise choice," I said, "but why leave all that culture in New York?"

"Well, the last year we lived up there we were robbed twice and mugged once," she said. "That did it. I decided to get out."

While establishing our individual pedigrees, I learned that they had lived in Oradell, New Jersey. I recalled that Oradell was also the hometown of one of our astronauts, Walter Shirra, who went into space in 1962. (I was living there at the time and would gladly have gone with him to get out of New Jersey.)

"Yes, we're very proud of Wally Shirra," said the husband.

"And understandably so," I said. "But he sure picked a heck of a way to get out of New Jersey, didn't he?"

"How's that?" the man asked.

"Took a space ship, Mercury 8. Talk about desperate," I said.

The female sipped her coffee, raised her painted eyebrows, and said, "Well, I still miss the culture in New York."

"Yeah, I reckon so. But you don't miss them robbers and muggers a whole helluva' lot, do you, ma'am?" I asked.

"Well, let me put it this way, we're not planning to move back," she said.

I thought about 'em all the way home. I'm gonna have to invite 'em to a cane grindin' or a peanut boilin', I reckon. It's a shame they're not takin' advantage of what culture we do have here, right?

Rednecks Are Some of History's Greatest Fighters

Who were the greatest fighting men in history? You are about to find out, thanks to an in-depth study on the subject, a copy of which was given to me by my friend, Nelson Carswell, Jr.

There are four groups of warriors who stand treetop tall above all others. They are: the Japanese samurai warriors; the famed

Gurkha soldiers of India; the fierce Cossacks of Russia; and, last but not least, any group of South Georgia rednecks.

You are undoubtedly familiar with the feats of the first three, so I'll confine this epistle to the latter group, the hell-raising, back-slapping, beer drinking, ear biting, pickup truck driving, good ole boys from Georgia below the city of Macon, who come into this world looking for trouble and exit the same way—usually after finding it.

If you took one fellow from each of the aforementioned groups and put them in a big sack and shook them up, there would be one heck of a fight. But you can bet your tire tool that the redneck would come out of the sack the winner and then look for someone to thank for inviting him to the party.

Don't think for a minute that rednecks are not an agreeable and friendly bunch. Quite the contrary; some of their greatest fights are among friends.

Here are recorded examples that tell the true story of these fantastic fighters:

In the War Between the States (labeled the Civil War by Yankees and left-of-center historians) these Southern commandos were hardly represented, but had they been I'm sure the outcome would have been decidedly different. The reason they weren't in the war until the last was that nobody told them about it until it was almost over. They thought it was a war between the Yankees and the big planters' sons and they weren't invited.

By the time they discovered that anyone who wanted to could join up and fight Yankees, the Northern army had already captured Atlanta. So they formed a little army, trained on the outskirts of Willacoochee for about an hour and a half, and set out to find the Yankees.

Unfortunately, they didn't know where Atlanta was, and they walked all the way to Austin, Texas, before realizing that they were headed in the wrong direction. On the outskirts of Austin they met a squad of Mexican banditos who had a rather hard time explaining they weren't Yankees, then cut and ran for the border, never to be heard from again.

The rednecks then marched back to Pensacola, Florida, and still had not found the Yankees. They could stand the inactivity no longer, so they began to fight among themselves. They chose up sides and fought for three days until someone volunteered that they'd never get to fight the Yankees if they all died in Florida. So a ceasefire was called to ponder the problem.

Between longneck Buds, a decision was reached. Instead of bullets, the rednecks agreed to use chinaberries, and while a green chinaberry would leave a wicked blister when fired from a 30.06 rifle, the recipient would live to fight (Yankees) another day. A thirty-minute chinaberry picking truce was allowed, and the fight resumed. Historians still rate it as the greatest battle ever fought. Neither side would give in. Even today, there is a living memorial to this battle, a chinaberry forest so thick a snake can't crawl through it.

Just as the issue was drawing to a close, a message was received that the Yankees had left Atlanta and were marching on Macon.

Macon! They all knew where Macon was! The two little armies merged and raced for Macon, where they found the Rebel army fortifying the city for the Yankee attack. But defense wasn't their style. They by-passed Macon and headed north, meeting 10,000 of Sherman's troops near Forsyth. They closed ranks and charged, each wearing a big grin. For six days the 154 rednecks and 10,000 Yankees fought it out, after which the Yankees decided they really didn't want to go to Macon nohow, made a left turn, and went to Savannah. But the lowdown Yankee rascals told the rednecks Savannah was in New Jersey so the rednecks held a victory barbecue and went home the next day.

After the war ended and the Yankee troops went home, the Northern ladies were puzzled by the red welts on their husbands' backsides (It seems that in their haste to find and fight the Yankees, most of the rednecks forgot to put the bullets back in their rifles and fought the entire battle with chinaberries!).

Of course, I'm sure you are familiar with the one time these great soldiers refused to fight. I understand Napoleon offered 200 rednecks a dollar and a half apiece if they would whip Russia so he could stay in Paris. The rednecks jumped at the chance and started walking to Russia via Alaska. They walked all the way to Little Rock, Arkansas, before a kindred spirit told them they had no beer, moonshine, country music, white socks, nor Levi Garrett chewing tobacco in Russia. So they agreed that money wasn't everything in the world and turned around and went home to South Georgia.

This may well have been a dark day in their history, but as re-

cently as the Vietnam War the redneck spirit again came to the
fore. Twenty-eight of their finest volunteered to land in China and
whip everything from there to Saigon. The army agreed, and
plans were in the making to land three pickups in China when the
war ended. To this day, people in South Georgia swear that both
sides heard about the plan and quit.

A South Georgia redneck will fight anyone but two people: his
father, because if he ever hit his father the old man would be honor
bound to kill him; and his mother, because she's the only one who
can whip his daddy, and she's the one who keeps the old man off
his back.

Buster's "Coming Out" Is Cause for Celebration

I don't go to as many parties as I once did, for two reasons. I'm
not invited to many, and the ones I go to turn into affairs where
sandwiches and friends are cut into little pieces.

Also, when you're single you tend to be a fifth wheel on the
party circuit. Sort of like a third for checkers, if you get what I
mean.

I have a married friend who says, "Parties? I avoid 'em like the
plague. Going to a party with your wife is like going fishing with
the game warden."

But his wife has other thoughts on the subject, like recently
when they were contemplating one. "Besides," he alibied,
"what'll I wear to a costume party?"

"Go sober," she suggested. "That'll fool everybody."

There are people who would brave a hurricane to get to a party,
any party, invited or not, like the gate crasher to whom any party
is a challenge.

The story goes that one walked through the door big as Ike and
enjoyed the hors d'oeuvres and the ladies for some ten minutes
before being confronted by a dignified gentleman who asked,
"And just who are you?"

The crasher beamed, sipped on his drink, and replied confi-
dently, "I'm with the groom."

"Oh, yeah? Well, I've got news for you, son," said the gentleman. "This is a wake!"

Most parties are identifiable by name—engagement party, birthday party, anniversary party, retirement party, cocktail party, pool party, bon voyage party, New Year's Eve party, etc. Once in a while, though, a fellow can wind up at a party that really ain't what he thought it was gonna' be. It happened to me once at a place down on the Altamaha between Lyons and Baxley, and them folks straight know how to throw a party down between Lyons and Baxley.

I was strolling past the drug store in downtown Lyons (the drug store *is* downtown Lyons) when I heard a voice bleat out, "Hey, Bo! Whatcha doin' in town?"

The bleater was a long-time acquaintance and third-generation bootlegger named Bobby Joe (no last names, please).

"Just dropped in for a couple of days to visit my mother. How's it goin', Bobby Joe?" I replied as I side-stepped tobacco juice and boiled peanut hulls.

"Fine as frog hair split three ways," he allowed. "Goin' to th' party t'nite?"

"Party? Where? What kinda' party?" I asked.

"Comin' out party for Bubba Bridges' young'un. Hell, ever'-body's gonna' be there. Got a band an' ever'thing," Bobby Joe said.

"Band? Who's playin', Bobby Joe?"

"Roscoe an' th' Tornadoes. You 'member them, don'tcha? They played at Sonny Sikes' weddin' reception at Bubba's place on th' river when ol' Sonny shot Popeye Crawford in th' foot for dancin' too close to his new bride, Margie Sue," Bobby Joe explained.

"Right! An' Roscoe stuck his guitar pick in Popeye's ear after Bubba broke a 20-20 wine bottle over his head an' Shotgun Lunceford thowed him in th' Altamaha," I recalled.

"Right, same band, only now they got Louella Blassingame singin' with 'em. You 'member Louella, don'tcha? She's the ol' gal what got kicked out o' th' church choir for singin' her own rock version of "Beulah Land" durin' th' revival one night after stoppin' off at Bubba's on th' way to th' church."

"Yeah, I remember Louella all right. She's the one that showed up at th' football field one night in a sun dress to sing "The Star Spangled Banner" an' th' officials forgot all about th' kickoff. You goin' to th' party?"

"Shoot I reckon! I ain't never missed a comin' out party at Bubba's," he said. "Y'cangoithmefyawanna."

Bobby Joe picked me up in his four-wheel drive about dark and we headed for the Altamaha and Bubba's place. A crowd had already gathered.

"By the way, Bobby Joe, what's Bubba's daughter's name, anyhow?" I asked as we walked toward the front door on a path lined with whitewashed tires.

"Daughter? Bubba ain't got no daughter. Four boys," he explained.

"But you said this was a comin' out party for one of Bubba's young'uns, didn't you?"

"It is. It's a comin' out party for Buster, his youngest boy. He just come out of Lewisburgh this mornin' after doin' a pair o' fives—five for possession of paraphanaliar to manufacture illegal likker an' five for sellin' it after he made it. This here's a big day for Bubba 'cause th' still ain't run a day since Buster's been gone. Not a drop," Bobby Joe said with obvious anticipation. "Besides, I ain't worked a lick m'sef in thirty-eight months an' it's been rough. Shore good t' have Buster back."

We walked through the front door only to be greeted by Louella Blassingame, sitting behind a table.

"Six dollars an' hold y'r han' out an' I'll stamp it. No cussin' on th' dance floor an' tips f'r th' sanger is 'prechated. You carryin' a pistol?" she asked.

"No ma'am, I swear I . . . " I began.

"No sweat. Take th' first door t' th' right an' y'can rent one from Bubba—dollar an hour. Y'all have a good time, ya' heah?"

Comin' out party for one o' Bubba's young'uns? You can count on it, 'bout once ever thirty-eight months!

An Update on Ol' Robbie Nail Bail

It's amazing how we run into people at the darndest places. Like last week when I stopped at the Yo-Ho Inn Beer Joint and Transmission Repair on U.S. 1 between Lyons and Baxley to make a telephone call. The last person in the world I expected to run into there was Robbie Nell Bell, from Alma ("Robbie Nail Bail, from Almer"), my old redneck friend.

I recognized Robbie Nail as soon as I entered the Yo-Ho Inn. She was shooting eight-ball with Boozer, and munching on a beef jerky. I was careful not to speak to her until the game was over. Robbie Nail "don't lack to be messed with" when she's shootin' pool.

She banked the eight ball in the side pocket, hung up her cue stick, and picked up a wrinkled dollar that Boozer had dropped on the table.

"Thanks, Turkey," she said to Boozer.

"Hey, Goat! Gimme a longneck Bud an' be dang sure it's cold," she said, dropping Boozer's buck on the bar.

"Y' ain't paid f'r that jerky yet," Goat said.

"Ain't goin' to, neither. Not as much money as I put in that jukebox an' cigarette machine. An' 'nother thang—if'n you don't lack it just say so an' I'll start goin' to th' Yeller Liver Bar on th' river," she threatened.

"Aw, Robbie Nail. I's jus' teasin', you know that," Goat said, almost apologetically.

"Ya' dang well better be. Hell, I've passed up better places 'n this lookin' f'r a ladies' room," she grumbled, moving toward the front door. "An' take that quarter change an' play Q-2, Goat."

I called to her just as she reached the door. "Hey! Robbie Nail!"

She turned, spotted me standing by the telephone, and tossed her empty longneck Bud bottle in the general direction of a trash can.

"Hey, newspaper man! Whut th' heck're ya' doin' daoun heah in God's country?" she asked.

"Oh, just passing through on my way back to Dublin," I told her. "What're you doing here? Last time I saw you, you were working at Mel's down near Broxton."

"Still do. I'm jus' up here f'r th' pageant Sat'day night in Lyons," she said.

"Pageant? What kind of pageant?"

"Miss Georgia Redneck. Havin' th' state finals at th' Red Barn Sat'day night," she said.

"Are you in it?"

"Dang right, good buddy. I'm representin' Region Four as Miss South Georgia Redneck," she boasted.

"Well! Congratulations, Robbie Nail! That's great and . . . "

"Shhhh! Don't call me that," she cautioned in a whisper.

"Why not? That's your name, right?"

"Yeah, right. But las' year's winner, Johnnie Faye Ramsey, said I'd be better off to use jus' one name. She won with "Faye" so I'm jus' usin' plain "Nail," O.K.?"

"Sure, fine. Nail it is," I promised.

"I 'prechate it. Now then . . . Hey, Goat! What happened to my dadgummed song? I tol' ya' to play Q-2 an' you played J-2. Wha's goin' on?" Robbie Nail demanded.

"I jus' made a mistake."

"Yeah? Well, you're gonna' make another'n if'n ya' don' put in 'nother quarter 'n play Q-2. Ya' heah that?" she warned.

In a matter of seconds the jukebox was blaring out with "Now I Lay Me Down to Cheat," by David Allen Coe.

"Jus' plain don' lack J-2," she mumbled.

"What is J-2?" I asked.

" 'Your Bedroom Eyes' by Vern Gosdin. Too sad. Makes me cry."

(I didn't pursue the point but couldn't help but muse on what she'd said. I'd give my twelve-string guitar, two Webb Pierce albums, and a Merle Haggard tape to see Robbie Nail Bail cry.)

I inquired further into the Region Four Miss Redneck Pageant.

"Where was the pageant held, Robbie Nail?"

"In Raymond Braswell's cow barn 'bout three miles out fum Broxton."

"Was it a beauty contest, or what?" I asked.

"Partly, but the mos' important thang was the talent. Least tha's what th' judges said."

"Who won the talent competition?"

"I did. Tha's th' main reason I'm here," she bragged.

"What'd you do, sing?"

"Sang? Hell, I can't sang. I changed all four tires on Junior Blakely's stock car and filled 'er up with gas in twenty-three seconds flat. New record," she said.

"Well, didn't Mildred Walters win last year?"

"Yeah . . . but she got disqualified during the questioning this year."

"Disqualified? Why?"

"Oh, one o' them smart aleck judges ast her right in front of

ever'body how often she procrastinated, an' that done it, friend,"
Robbie Nail explained.

"What do you mean? What did Mildred do?"

"Do? She flattened that sucker with a right and then stomped
on his face till th' sheriff stopped her. An' I tell you, I don't blame
her a dadgummed bit. We didn' none of us get in th' pageant to be
insulted."

They Got Rednecks Up'n North Georgia Too

Don't think for a minute that all the rednecks are confined to
such South Georgia locales as Waycross, Ludowici, Baxley, Wila-
coochee, Hinesville, Nahunta, Broxton, and points south. You
can bet your six-pack of Pabst Blue Ribbon, pickup, and two
packs of Red Man on that. North Georgia's got 'em, too, Hoss.
Here's how I found out.

When I left Gatlinburg on Labor Day morning I had my heart
set on lunching at the famous Smith House in Dahlonega. I was in
such a hurry to get there that I only stopped once, at the ranger
station in Vogel State Park, for the pause that refreshes. I also had
a Coke, but no luck with my planned Smith House lunch. I should
have had dinner there on the way up on Friday. The Smith House
is closed on Mondays. You might want to make a note of same and
stick it on your refrigerator door for future reference.

While the Smith House is closed on Mondays, Buddy's Grill
and Souvenir Shop, twelve miles south of Dahlonega on Georgia
60 near Murrayville, is wide open, baby. Ol' Buddy hasn't closed
since prohibition ended. (Trust me, Jimmy!)

So I pulled in at Buddy's and parked between a pickup and a
Jeep, then hesitated briefly at the entrance to read the welcome
sign: "No Shoes—No Shirt—No Service." I realized then and
there that I wasn't about to enter the Pleasant Pheasant or Nikolai's Roof.

Inside, I sat at the counter and listened to some invisible character moan and groan from the jukebox some sad sonnet about his
wife running off with the hired help, leaving him with four kids
and this problem: "I'm a stranger in the kitchen 'cause I never
spent much time in there."

The front booth, undoubtedly a prestige seat, was occupied by something wearing dirty sneakers and what was once a white T-shirt. Remember the sign on the front door? Well, it contained no stipulation that the shoes and shirt be clean—just on. "It" was eating lunch, a Buddyburger, French fries, and a "Meller Yeller." Now then, you just can't hardly get a lunch like that at the Smith House, Pleasant Pheasant, or Nikolai's Roof (or basement, for that matter).

I listened as the waitress, Linda, who may be the one who does "Its" laundry, conversed.

"Didja' git drunk Sat'dy nite, Billy Joe?" she asked.

"Shoot, I reckon! Me'n Joe B. went to th' dance over at Chestnut Mountain. Got home 'bout daylight," Billy Joe replied. "Lordy, I felt some kind o' bad Sunday mornin'."

"Who'd y'all take?"

"Didn' take nobody. Why take one cracker when y'can go by y'sef an' hav' a shot at th' whole box?"

"Betcha' didn' git up til' dinner time Sunday, didja'?" Linda giggled.

"Betcha I did, too. Y'see Mama's got this rule that it don't make no diff'rence how drunk I git Sat'dy nite, I still gotta' git up an' go with her to Sunday School an' church Sunday mornin'," Billy Joe explained.

(Hooray for Billy Joe's mama!)

"Heck, my Daddy's 'bout as bad," Linda countered. "I got two young'uns an' been livin' to home since me'n Roscoe split up las' year an' Daddy makes me git my tail outta' bed an' git to work no matter how late I stay out. He says long's I live in his house I'm gonna do lak he says."

(Hooray for Linda's daddy!)

Linda then dropped one of her infrequent tips in the jukebox and pushed a button, thereby activating a previously dormant Willie Nelson who was having problems of his own and bellowed them out for me, Buddy, Billy Joe, Linda, and the world to hear: "Maybe I didn't love you—quite as often as I should have; you're always on my mind."

I paid Buddy, Billy Joe burped, and I left.

Rednecks? I'll just tell you this, good buddy. Those critters are everywhere.

For Pete's Sake—Anything!

Occasionally, it's best to keep your mouth shut. Like when you're in a strange juke joint in a strange county, surrounded by, what else? Strangers. Big, muscular strangers. Half-loaded strangers that don't cotton to other strangers.
What was I doing there in the first place?
I was riding my Harley Davidson back to Dublin from Statesboro after visiting with my daughter and stopped in the joint to buy cigarettes and make a phone call. Needing change for both, I paused at the cash register. The "proprietor" was busy shooting pool.
"Whatcha' need, Hoss?" he asked.
"Change for a dollar," I replied.
"Hep y'sef, the register's open. I trust everybody but if I ketch a feller beatin' me, I shoot him," he said, banking the three ball in the side pocket.
I opened the cigarettes and put a dime in the phone. Busy. I had a choice, kill flies or watch the pool game. I climbed on a stool to watch.
"If y' wanna beer or somethin', the Buds ain't cold," he said, missing a three ball combination and cursing. (The "somethin'" turned out to be Pepsi and orange.)
The big guy walked in just as I opened a Pepsi. Did I say big? He'd have to curl up to lie down in a box car.
"That yore big ol' Harley out front?" he asked as he reached in the cooler and pulled out a long-neck Bud.
"Yeah, right. Uh, say . . . the Bud ain't cold."
"Ain't cold! Hey, Snake! How come this Bud ain't cold?" he bellowed.
"'Cause Roy didn't bring it 'til dinner time, tha's why," Snake explained after spotting the eight ball. "He gits sorrier ever' day, Pete."
Reluctantly, Pete exchanged the hot Bud for a cold Miller.
"Where's Nell at, Snake?" he demanded.
"In the back. Want her?"
"Yeah! Tell her to git her tail out here and fix me somethin' to eat," Pete growled. (My tail was already out there. All he had to do was say the word. I'd have jumped the counter and fired up the grill before you could say Paul Bunyan.)

Enter Nell, as enthusiastic as a George McGovern delegate as she played "find the apron strings" and yawned.

"Whatch' wanna eat?" she grunted.

"Whatever you got that don't bite back," he answered, flipping a quarter in her general direction. "Play J-3 and L-8."

Pete moved toward the door, another Miller in hand. "Come on, let's take another look at that ol' Harley."

Waylon, Willie, and the boys (J-3) wailed on, extolling the virtues of beer drinking in Luckenbach, Texas. As we left, Kenny Rogers (L-8) profiling the untimely exodus of some woman named Lucille followed.

Pete tossed the empty Miller in the back of a red pickup occupied by a bulldog and many long-neck Bud bottles, dead soldiers from previous beer battles.

"Better watch it, Erk," he belched.

"Your dog?" I asked.

"Yeah, and he ain't worth a damn for nothin', just like me."

He kicked a leg and straddled the Harley. Ever seen a rhinoceros on a skate board? You get the picture.

"Had me one o' these back in the sixties. Ol' Harley 74. Keep thinking' 'bout gittin' another 'un. You ride much?"

"Yeah, all the time. Wanna' ride it?" I asked.

"You mean it?"

"Be my guest, Pete."

(His next statement grabbed me.)

"Ain't rode since I wrecked mine," he said.

"What happened?" I asked with more than passing interest.

"Aw, I got drunk one night and run over a tractor-trailer outside of Claxton. Broke my leg and a few ribs. A feller' oughtn't to ride 'em when he's drunk," he philosophized.

"Right! I'll drink to that!"

"You shore you don't care?"

I lied. I just plain lied.

"Naw, go ahead. You're big enough to handle it." (Big enough? Hell, he could pick it up and tote it!)

And away he went.

I shared the tailgate of Pete's pickup with Erk and waited. I wondered lots of things, like, "Why did I do it?" "Why am I here?" "Will my insurance cover the motorcycle with Pete riding it?" Also, "Where in heck did Pete come up with a name like Erk?" I'd ask him when, and if, he returned.

The air was shattered by the hoarse voice of Nell coming from the juke joint door.

"Where's Pete at?" she boomed.

"He's ridin' my motorcycle," I replied.

"Well, when he gits back tell him to git his tail in here and eat!" Erk did his only trick. He played dead, having heard Nell's bark many times before, no doubt. He continued his trick until Pete roared up minutes later.

"Man! That was fun! I shore appreciate the ride. I'm just gonna' have to git me another 'un," Pete vowed.

"Good. Oh, Nell said your dinner's ready."

"Yeah . . . O.K. Come on and let's eat," he said.

Inside, Pete pulled up a stool to a cow and a few bushels of potatoes and dumped about a gallon of ketchup on the whole she-bang.

"Where's my tea at, Nell?" he asked.

"Ain't got no tea. You wanna' beer?"

"Naw, gimme' a couple of Pepsis and a glass o' water."

Erk stretched out in front of the jukebox and waited, along with Waylon and Kenny. Shortly, Pete flipped him a piece of the cow.

"Where'd you come up with a name like Erk, Pete?" I asked.

"Named him after Erk Russell at Georgia. Can't call no dog Erskine so I call him Erk," he explained. "I found him down at the junk yard."

"You a Georgia fan, Pete?"

"Well, I don't exactly run out and buy a new flea collar or stand on one leg when they play, but I like 'em. I seen 'em play last year in Jacksonville. Them junkyard dogs was somethin'! They'll bust your head in, good buddy," he said between bites.

Pete flipped another quarter at Nell. Words were unnecessary. She dropped it in the jukebox and punched J-3 and L-8. Erk got up and relocated by the cigarette machine.

I figured this was where I came in.

"Well, I guess I better hit the road," I said, easing off my stool.

"Yeah? Well, thanks for the ride and . . . say, where you from?" Pete asked.

"Dublin. I'm from Dublin, Pete."

"You work in Dublin?"

"Right. I write for the newspaper. The *Dublin Courier Herald*," I said.

"Oh, yeah? Whadda' you write?" Pete asked.

"I write a column, mostly about people. Might even write a column 'bout you, Pete."

Nell was resurrected long enough to offer this word of caution.

"Last time somebody wrote 'bout Pete he got in trouble," she said. "Feller from Savannah wrote 'bout him making liquor and his big brother didn't like it. He found him and whupped up on him," she said before returning to her tomb.

"Yeah, you better be careful. My brother worked the feller over pretty good. Broke his back and messed up his face," Pete related.

I was near the door and all set to depart. I listened REAL closely to what Pete was saying.

"Well, see y'all later," I called back as I opened the door.

I had turned the lights on and shifted into first gear when I heard Pete yelling from the doorway.

"I'll be watchin' for yore paper! Oh, yeah, what's yore name, anyway?"

"Name's Hall! Doug Hall! But I write my column under the name of Whaley, Bo Whaley. Tell your big brother he can find it on page two!"

Robbie Nail Is Doing Quite Well

I'm pleased to report that Robbie Nail is quite well. She quit her waitress job at Mel's Juke, located about a six-pack north of Broxton, had the water pump fixed on her '73 Ford and moved to Nashville.

She writes country songs (most a sort of autobiography) and is now in the country music business full-time.

She called (collect) from Nashville one Saturday night after the Grand Ole Opry from a Nashville spot called the Ace of Spades.

"How in the world are you, Robbie Nail?" I asked.

"Fine, Chief, jus' fine," she said. "Writin' country songs an' makin' money faster'n a bootlegger. Even think' 'bout gittin' married agin soon's my boyfriend, Roy, gits his d'vorce from that ol' Margie."

"Well, congratulations. What took you to Nashville?" I asked.

"Y 'member that song I wrote that Bobby an' th' Rattlesnakes recorded in Waycross 'bout two years ago, 'Papa Died and Mama Cried, 'Cause the Insurance Had Done Lapsed'?"

"Right, I remember. A real tear-jerker," I said.

"Wail, that's whut started th' whole thaing," she said. "Roy, tha's my boyfriend, heard it an' his band, Roy's Ramblers, recorded it. Roy done th' saingin', naturally, an' it became a big hit. So now, I write 'em an' Roy saings 'em. He gives me seven dollars f'r ever one I write."

"I'm proud of you. Have you written very many?" I asked.

"Shoot I reckon! A whole 'baccer sheet full," she bellowed. "I had a real big 'un right after Thanksgiving las' year when my brother's wife run off with th' Roto-Rooter man."

"What was the name of it?"

"You mean you ain't heard it? It's called, 'I Stuffed Her Turkey and She Cooked My Goose,'" she said. "I tell you what, I'll jus' send all of 'em down to you an' you can be my Georgia agent. How 'bout that?" she giggled.

"Great! Send 'em on down. You have lots of fans in this area," I told her.

I'm not sure you're ready for this, but here is the list of songs written by Robbie Nail Bail, fum Almer, that arrived in the morning mail:

- "When I'm Alone I'm in Bad Company."
- "A Sad Song Don't Care Whose Heart It Breaks"
- "I Wouldn't Take Her to a Dogfight, but I Know She'd Win if I Did"
- "I May Fall Again, but I'll Never Get Up This Slow"
- "You're the Busiest Memory in Town"
- "Your Face Is Familiar, but I Forget the Name"
- "You Don't Have to Go Home, Baby, but You Can't Stay Here"
- "It's Easy to Find an Unhappy Woman Till I Start Looking for Mine"
- "The More I Think of You, the Less I Think of Me"
- "Don't Cry Down My Back, Baby, You Might Rust My Spurs"
- "I Can't Afford to Half My Half Again"

- "The Bridge Washed Out, I Can't Swim, and My Baby's on the Other Side of the River"
- "Forever, For Us, Wasn't Nearly As Long As We Planned On"
- "I Got to Her House Just in Time to be Late"
- "I'm Afriad to Come Home Early Without Warning Her First"
- "My Wife Ran Off with My Best Friend—And I Sure Do Miss Him"
- "Send Her a Dozen Roses, and Pour Four for Me"
- "He's Walking in My Tracks, but He Can't Fill My Shoes"
- "She's Gone, and She Took Everything but the Blame"
- "I Can't Believe I Gave Up 'Good Mornin' Darling' and 'We Love You Daddy,' for This"
- "I'd Rather Be Picked Up Here Than to Be Put Down at Home"
- "When the Phone Don't Ring, You'll Know It's Me That Ain't Calling"
- "If You Want to Keep the Beer Real Cold, Put It Next to My Ex-Wife's Heart"
- "I Need Somebody Bad Tonight 'Cause I Just Lost Somebody Good Today"
- "The Score Is: Liars One—Believers Zero"
- "I'm Ashamed to Be Here, but Not Ashamed Enough to Leave"
- "How Can Six-year-old Whiskey Beat a Thirty-two-year-old Man?"
- "She's Waiting on Tables While Waiting for the Tables to Turn"
- "Now That She's Got Me Where She Wants Me, She Don't Want Me"
- "I Can't Even Do Wrong Right No More"
- "The Devil Is a Woman in a Short Red Dress"
- "She Ain't Much to See, but Looks Good Through the Bottom of a Glass"
- "I Done 'Bout Lived Myself to Death"
- "It's Bad When You Get Caught with the Goods"
- "Remember to Remind Me I'm Leaving"
- "It Took a Hell of a Man to Take My Ann, but It Sure Didn't Take Him Long to Do It"

- "Them What Ain't Got Can't Lose"
- "I'm Sick and Tired of Waking Up Sick and Tired"

Test Yourself: Are You a Redneck?

Are you a redneck? Want a sure-fire guide to find out? Take a look.

You're a redneck if:

- You harbor a continuing urge to slap somebody, stomp on somethin', or spit.
- You still wear a burr haircut, chew on kitchen matches, and constantly hope some long-hair will make fun of your white socks so you can break his fingers as sort of an in-house joke.
- You're certain that anybody who drives an old VW with a Solar Power or Anti-Nuke bumper sticker is a Commie pinko.
- You hope some guy from New Jersey will honk at you when the light turns green so you can crawl out of your pickup, give him a Confederate talkin' to, and embarrass him in front of his old lady.
- You think the only people who shouldn't wear boots are women.
- The only people you're afraid to sass are your mama and daddy and the only people your daddy is afraid to sass are his mama and daddy.
- You wonder why all them people in coats and ties are going into Katz's Deli when the beer joint is right across the street.
- You wear white shirts, with snaps instead of buttons, with a little embroidery on them, and your bellybutton shows.
- You think all bars should have pickled eggs instead of hanging plants and you've boozed it up at Scoot Inn, the Horseshoe Lounge, the Manchaca Bar and Dry Gulch Watering Hole but couldn't find the Veranda, Wylie's, or the Inn Place with a Rand-McNally guide.
- You think the president should stop busing, nuke Iran, reinstate the draft, eliminate welfare, and re-activate CCC camps to try and make things as miserable as they were when you were a kid so children these days can develop some character.
- You can't stand Shakespeare, poetry, ballet, or plays, but love

the chase scenes on HBO and enjoy it when the sheriff in the movie swears a lot.

• You only watch the Indy 500 to see the wrecks and cars blowing up.

• You think Bella Abzug and Jane Fonda ought to "jest shut the hell up," but Dolly Parton, bless her little ol' pea-pickin' heart, can say anything she wants to as far as you're concerned.

• The only time you hold a woman's chair is to keep from falling down at the Dry Gulch on Saturday night.

• You sign up for the draft and take your own mug with you only to learn they ain't signin' up for free beer.

• You never miss a civil rights rally and stand across the street and sing "Dixie" at the top of your voice.

• You swallow tobacco juice as a joke and can spit over an eight rail fence.

• You wouldn't own a shirt that didn't have two pockets.

• You can strike a match on your britches or with your thumbnail, can whistle through your teeth, and have your name burned on your belt.

• You prop your foot in the booth at the diner, dump cigarette ashes in the saucer, and wouldn't look at a menu if your life depended on it, preferring to tell the waitress, "jus' bring me two aigs done hard an' some o' them sausages. Lots o' grits."

• You ain't no golfer but "par for the course" is a blonde, a redhead, and a brunette over the weekend.

• The last newspaper you read was the one in which you advertised your four-wheel drive pickup for sale with "call for Bubba at the Dry Gulch Watering Hole between 9:00 P.M. and 3:00 A.M., Friday and Saturday."

• You've done a little time in Reidsville for "salt and battry" and still carry a teaspoon in your belt.

• You can roll a cigarette in the back of a pickup going sixty miles per hour between Brewton and Minter.

So? What's the verdict?

Robbie Nail's Going for a Triple Dose of Husband

On a recent trip to Waycross, I stopped off at Mel's Juke, about a six-pack north of Broxton, for a barbecue sandwich. Robbie

Nail was formerly the head waitress and bouncer at Mel's before she hit the big time and moved off "up yonder to Nashville to write country songs."

Mel broke the news.

"Where's Robbie Nail?" I asked.

"Still up north," Mel said. "She's gonna' git married again in July," Mel said. "Marryin' a good ol' boy fum over Douglas way. Name's Urel Simpson (properly pronounced 'You-rail Seeumpson' in Melanese). Kinda' nice that their names rhyme, ain't it? Y'know, Robbie Nail and You-rail?"

"Yeah, nice," I agreed. "Where's the weddin' gonna' be, Mel?"

"In the reposin' room at Seeumpson's Funeral Home, where You-rail works in the daytime," Mel said.

"Where You-rail works in the daytime? What about at night? Does he work at night?" I asked.

"Tha's a big ten-four."

"Where? Where does he work at night?"

"Well, he don't talk 'bout that," Mel said.

"Oh, I see. Has You-rail been married before?"

"Yeah, once't. Right in that same reposin' room, too. Married a woman wrestler fum Jacksonville. I was bes' man an' like his daddy said after th' weddin', 'he shore looked natural.'"

"I'll bet he did. Will there be a reception after the wedding, Mel?"

"Doggone right! Havin' it rat cheer like we've always done whenever Robbie Nail got married," Mel said with pride.

"You got enough room? Looks a little small to me," I said.

"Got plenty o' room. You-rail's borrowin' a tent from the funeral home to set up out by th' barbecue pit. An' cheers, too. His uncle, what owns the funeral home, tol' him he could have all th' cheers he needed, provided of course they won't no funeral that day," Mel allowed. "Ya' want 'nother samich?"

"No thanks. One's just enough. Good, too," I told him. "Say, Mel, you heard from Robbie Nail lately?"

"Kinda' second-hand, I have. She called my mama fum Nashville las' week to talk about th' weddin' an' th' reception. You know, woman talk," he said.

"Yeah, like what to serve, how many people to invite, and all that," I suggested.

"Right, an' th' honeymoon," Mel said, "Can't fergit th' honeymoon."

"Where are they goin'?"

"Well, I kinda' figger they'll go to Jaykull. Robbie Nail always goes to Jaykull on her honeymoons. 'Course, now if'n they's a funeral the day o' th' weddin' they ain't goin' nowhere 'cept to th' Shady Oaks Motel over on Highway 86," Mel allowed.

"Why not? What's a funeral got to do with Robbie Nail and You-rail's honeymoon?"

"It's got ever'thing to do with it," Mel said. "You-rail ain't got no car so he's plannin' on usin' th' hearse to take Robbie Nail to Jaykull."

"No car? Where's his car?" I asked.

"Ain't got one. Has somethin' to do with his night work," Mel said. "Th' GBI caught him down close to Blackshear and took it. Gonna' be sold at a auction next month. Dang good car, too. A '81 Trans-Am, with overdrive an' everything. I rode with him fum Douglas to Tifton 'bout six months ago an' that sucker'll straight fly!"

"So, everything is all set? For the reception, I mean."

"Yeah, Mama's headin' th' food an' I'm handlin' th' drinks," Mel said.

"You planning on serving things like caviar, herring, and anchovies?"

"Naw, I ain't servin' no wine. Jus' longneck Bud an' Colt 45, with some Meller Yeller f'r th' younguns," Mel said.

Is Robbie Nail for real? You bet your pickup she's for real—and so's Mel, who runs his juke joint about a six-pack north of Broxton.

Sally's Gonna' Party All Night Long

Like you, I know revelers who wouldn't stay home Friday and Saturday nights if you chained them to the refrigerator. They'd drag that frost-free sucker right on down to their favorite night spot and "get it on," with the box dragging behind.

On the other hand, there are those who wouldn't vacate the confines of their den and TV if the house caught fire.

Take Sally, for instance. She's a flat (well, not really) goin' out gal.

As the office clock approaches 5:00 P.M. any Friday, Sally starts boogying in her desk chair while finger-tapping on her desk top. And when the big hand reaches twelve and the little hand is on five, watch out! She exits the office like a speed skater, does the Michael Jackson moon walk through the parking lot, and slides under the steering wheel of her little compact gas saver.

Does Sally start the engine, back out, and dig off right away? Hardly. First things first. She turns the radio on, predialed to her favorite station, lights up a Salem Light 100, and *then* backs out and boogies all the way home, the steering wheel replacing her desk top.

From 5:13 P.M. until 7:00 P.M., Sally takes care of her young'un, whips up a little supper, bathes, slips (Oops! Excuse me, tugs and struggles) into clean jeans, and drops the dirty dishes in the sink—all done while she guzzles a beer and listens to the pregame warm-up that blasts from her AM-FM radio stereo cassette tape player, the only household item, other than the young'un, that she insisted on keeping when her lawyer drew up the divorce agreement after she and Paul split.

About 7:30 P.M., Sally's baby sitter shows up and it's Friday night game time.

Actually, Sally's Friday night out *really* begins the moment she steps out of her front door and trips the light fantastic en route to her car, shouting "Yaaaahhhoooo! Gonna' party ALL night long! Le's git it on, baby!"

If, by chance, you've never seen the jeans-clad Sallys of this world in action on the "daintz" floor Friday and Saturday nights, you really ain't lived a full life. And believe me, it's a crying shame what the Sallys put those little pieces of denim through with all their twistin' an' shakin'.

Like my good friend Buttercup Hill, from Route 3, Baxley, says: "If Sally don't start a fire in your basement, your wood's wet."

Then, there's ol' Claude. He hits the goin' out trail on Friday and Saturday nights, too, lookin' for the Sallys of the night beat. And Claude's a loner.

"Shoot! I ain't takin' no girl to no dance. I sorta' like to m'neuver 'round, m'sef," he allows.

You can spot Claude in a flash. He just sorta' rolls inside the place, swaying from side to side, and has more chains hanging around his neck than Houdini. And his shirt is open to his belly-button so they can be seen. He strolls straight to the bar, leans on it, lights a Winston, and commences to survey the pickin's. He's lookin' for Sally.

Once he spots her, does he approach Sally and say, "Pardon me, would you like to dance?"

Negatory. Ol' Claude's smooth-as-Black-Velvet-approach runs something like, "Gitcha' tail up, gal, an' le's git it on 'fore I change my mind."

Although Claude may look like Buddy Hackett, smell like the Goat Man, and dance like Dr. Frankenstein's monster, in his mind he looks like Robert Redford, smells like Boy George, and dances like Michael Jackson.

Claude's strictly a goin' out man who wouldn't stay home on Friday and Saturday night if he knew Sally was on the way over (skin-tight jeans an' all) with a five-gallon bucket full of daiquiri's, a case of longneck Bud, three Alabama tapes, and divorce papers three days old.

"Might miss somethin'," Claude would say.

Miss somethin'?

What, pray tell? What, Claude?

Redneck Stories Are in Plentiful Supply

Hardly a week passes without somebody writing or telling me a story about rednecks. Everybody is a self-styled expert on the subject. I've even received redneck stories from people in Brooklyn, New York, and from as far away as Australia.

Apparently people's knowledge of rednecks comes from television and liberal newspapers. Nevertheless, here are some of the many thoughts about rednecks I've received over the years from folks far removed from the Southland.

• It's difficult to recognize a redneck—he usually covers it with a hood.

• I just bought the world's thinnest book: *The History of Redneck Culture.*

• Why do redneck haircuts cost eight dollars? (Answer: Because the barber charges two dollars per corner.)

• An old farmer and his wife were leaning on the fence at their hogpen when the old lady wistfully murmured, "Tomorrow's our golden wedding anniversary, Luther. Let's kill the pig."

Luther pondered the suggestion, removed a stick match from his mouth, spit over the fence, and wearily replied, "What's the use of murdering a pig for somethin' that happened fifty years ago?"

• A southern gentleman is a redneck with money in the bank.

• The old redneck was watching the storekeeper unwrap a shipment of brightly colored men's pajamas at the country store.

"What's that?" he asked.

"Pajamas, Homer," replied the storekeeper.

"What are they for?"

"You wear them at night," the storekeeper explained. "Wanna buy a pair?"

"Nope," said the old redneck. "Don't go nowhere at night 'cept to bed."

• While waiting for their clothes to dry at the local laundrymat, two redneck wives were discussing the problem of getting their husbands up in time to go to work.

"How do you get Bubba outta' bed in the mornin'?" asked Betty June.

"Well," replied Bertha Mae, "ah jus' open th' bedroom door and throw th' cat in."

"Does that git him up?" Betty June asked.

"It shore do," Bertha Mae replied. "He sleeps with th' dawg."

• A redneck on his way fishing stopped in at a bait shop to buy some worms.

"How much are y'r worms?" he asked the owner.

"On special today," the owner said. "All you want for a dollar."

"Good. Gimmee two dollars' worth."

• A redneck accompanied his wife to a PTO meeting at the elementary school. During the meeting, a proposal was made to buy a gondola to put in the lake in front of the school.

The redneck liked the idea so much that he stood up and proposed with enthusiasm, "I think that's a great idea! Let's git two—a male and a female!"

• The redneck girl was very upset and said to her friend, "I'm so mad, Patty Sue, I could jus' spit!"

"Why? What's wrong?" asked Patty Sue.

"Aw, that Bobby Joe ast me t' marry him las' night and . . ."

"Well, my Lord, Mamie Ruth, what's so wrong with that?"

"Well, it's like this heah. My Mama married my Daddy, my Grandma married my Grandpa, my aunt married my uncle, my uncle married my aunt—so why should I marry a complete stranger?"

• The redneck husband gave his wife a washing machine for Christmas but had to return it. Why? Every time she got in it she came out black and blue.

The redneck story well never runs dry . . .

Part 2

Bonafide Americans
Are for Real, Too

I have long believed that many of America's best and most loyal citizens inhabit the country's small towns. I'm talking about towns so small that everybody knows everybody else's birthday, most shoe sizes, who's taking what medication for what malady, what the neighbors had for supper the night before, and most telephone numbers by heart.

I'm talking real bonafide Americans here. Folks who return library books before they're due, pay bills on time and frequently with cash, view credit cards with disdain, and consider NASA to be a child's negative reply to an adult's question.

I'm talking folks who talk to God as a personal friend as opposed to a parole officer, cry real tears at the funerals of friends, display real concern for anybody who has to go to the hospital, take in stray dogs and cats, patch pants and turn shirt collars, go to PTO meetings to better the school for the kids' sake, give to worthy causes without fanfare, work with their hands, and love with their hearts.

Yes, I'm talking bonafide Americans here.

If asked to profile one person whom I would characterize as a real bonafide American I would turn without hesitation to "Mr. Wes," affectionately referred to by most who knew him as "Uncle Wes."

As a boy growing up, I thought the man must have had more nieces and nephews than anybody in the world. To one and all, male and female, young and old, he was "Uncle Wes."

Small of stature with a trademark handlebar moustache, Uncle Wes lived in the almost unheard of town of Powelton, a village in North Georgia near Athens, home of the University of Georgia. He operated a small (very small) country store. Prior to his death in 1944 at age seventy-four, his inventory was probably never larger than what could be placed in two of today's shopping carts. Accounting and bookkeeping never were problems for Mr. Wes. He made change from his pocket and, to my knowledge, never had a bank account. Bills? He always paid cash. And he chewed tobacco, Brown's Mule chewing tobacco, regularly. He is the only man I've ever known who could chew tobacco, eat parched peanuts, and drink a Coca-Cola at the same time.

My father told and re-told what I consider a classic story about Mr. Wes. He loved to tell it, especially at Christmas time when all Mr. Wes's family would come to visit. I heard the story told dozens of times. I can neither vouch for nor discount its authenticity. I never questioned my father about it, but I will concede that he was a great storyteller sometimes prone to taking simple facts that would otherwise prove dull and inflating them to the point where he could hold a listener spellbound. I am inclined to think that was true in the case of Mr. Wes and the story he told about him so often.

Here's the story. You be the judge.

A Dr. Jekyll and Mr. Hyde Hospital Patient

MR. WES, AT AGE SIXTY-FIVE, was admitted to the hospital for the first time in his life. In fact, until then he had never found it necessary to visit a doctor. He was very healthy, and illness had been completely foreign to him. Nevertheless, he was determined to be the ideal patient and cooperated with nurses and the hospital to the fullest.

When it was time to have his blood pressure taken, he would have his pajama sleeve rolled up before the nurse arrived at his bedside to take it. When it was time to take his medicine, his mouth was open and ready. The same with X-rays. The same with feeding time, and he ate all the food recommended to him.

One morning, however, the nurse entered his room with medical chart in hand and announced, "Mr. Wes, since you have been quite 'irregular' for the past three days, the doctor has ordered that you be afforded some relief."

"Yes, ma'am. Whatever you say," he agreed. "Just tell me what you want me to do."

"You know something, Mr. Wes, you must be about the best and most cooperative patient we've ever had in this hospital," she replied.

"Well, I just want to make it as easy for you as I can because I know how busy you are."

"We all appreciate your attitude," she said. "Now don't tell the other patients, but you really are our favorite."

"Thank you."

"I'll be right back to give you some relief," she said.

(Note: Let it be recorded here and now that Mr. Wes had never in his life experienced an enema. It was as foreign to him as New York and San Francisco.)

Shortly, the nurse returned with her "apparatus" and said to Mr. Wes, "Now then, sugar, if you will just turn on your left side . . ."

"Yes, ma'am. I'll be glad to," he replied. And he did.

The nurse then reached underneath the sheet with the nozzle end of the "apparatus" in hand and started to make the necessary connection. However, at that point Mr. Wes whirled around on his back, and his right arm shot out like a rocket, knocking the nurse's glasses off. She caught them in her arms and shouted.

"Why, Mr. Wes! I'm surprised at you! Do you realize you almost broke my glasses!"

"To heck with your glasses! Do you know where you almost stuck that thing!"

Oh, I forgot to mention it but Mr. Wes was Wesley Whitfield Whaley, my grandfather. And when my father told the story, Mr. Wes would laugh louder than anybody. He never confirmed or denied the story. I think he didn't want to steal his oldest son's thunder.

Living Life in the Slow Lane

I'm amazed at the fast pace we maintain in today's world. It doesn't seem possible that I could have breakfast in Atlanta, lunch in New York, and dinner in Chicago; dial a few digits and in seconds talk to someone almost anywhere in the world; or watch a halfback sprint seventy-eight yards for a touchdown and then, via the miracle of instant replay, watch him do it again.

My computer astonishes me when it tells me I've hit the wrong key, inserted the wrong disk, or entered the wrong date to call up a file.

We move at a fast pace, at least most of us do, but there are those who still maintain a snail's pace in the slow lane. There's absolutely nothing wrong with that, but somehow I'm not ready for it when confronted by one of them, like the one I met just south of Chattanooga, Tennessee.

I was driving south on Interstate 75 toward Atlanta when I saw a sign: Chatsworth, Next Exit, 1 Mile."

"Why not?" I asked myself, so I exited and drove toward Chatsworth on U. S. Highway 76 to try to locate a fellow I hadn't seen or heard from since the early 1950s—thirty-five years ago—when we played professional baseball together. His name was Glenn Roberts, a first baseman. His wife was Wanda, a lovely girl. Glenn was a good friend and teammate, and a good first baseman.

I stopped and checked the telephone book outside an Amoco station. No Glenn Roberts. I went inside and asked the owner if he knew a Glenn Roberts. He told me there used to be one who lived in Chatsworth, but he moved to Dalton quite a few years back to work for Georgia Power. And yes, his wife was named Wanda.

As happens frequently, and can be verified by anyone who's ever ridden with me, I got on the wrong road when I left Chatsworth. Instead of U.S. 76 that would have taken me to Dalton, I somehow managed to get on Georgia 225 that would have taken me to Calhoun. I also can't read a map, so I began looking for somebody—anybody—to ask directions to Dalton.

Shortly, I spotted a country store reminiscent of country stores I knew in my boyhood—unpainted, an overhang from the roof, and signs of all kinds nailed on the outside walls. Seated on a wooden box, probably an apple box, out front was an elderly man. He had to be in his eighties and would have been a great subject for a Norman Rockwell *Saturday Evening Post* cover.

The man was small and had on a pair of well-worn Dee-Cee overalls, a blue work shirt with the collar buttoned but no tie, a denim jacket with elbow patches, an old brown felt hat, and high-top shoes, the kind made of very soft leather with about a two-inch-wide strip of elastic on the sides. His hands, like his face, were like leather, and he wore black horn-rimmed reading glasses like my grandpa used to buy at the five and ten for a quarter.

I imagined that he remembered prohibition and Al Capone, had voted for Franklin D. Roosevelt for President of the United States all four times, and had voted for Eugene Talmadge every time he ran. I also imagined that he could tell about the Great Depression, Pearl Harbor, and V-E and V-J day. He might even have had children or grandchildren who knew about all three firsthand and was probably just as shocked as the rest of us in August 1945 when the big one was dropped on Hiroshima.

I parked, got out of my car, and walked over to him confident that he could and would put me on the right road to Dalton.

"Excuse me, sir, but can you tell me what road I take to get to Dalton?" I asked.

"Yep, jus' go back up to the top o' th' hill an' take a right," he answered.

"I see, and how long will it take me to get there?"

"Don't rightly know. I ain't never been there, but I always wanted to go."

And how far was it? I checked. A grand total of nineteen miles, and the old gentleman "had never been there, but always wanted to go."

Maybe—just maybe—we're not moving at as fast a pace as I thought.

I pegged the old gentleman right away as a bonafide American.

A Tribute to a Great American

This is intended as a tribute to the memory of a friend, tried and true: Marshall Chapman, who died July 16, 1987. He was ninety-three when he died, but those numbers could have easily been reversed. He thought, lived, and laughed like a thirty-nine-year-old. Although he was thirty years my senior, I never enjoyed a friendship more.

I attended his funeral on a Saturday morning. It was simple and appropriate, dominated by dignity and wrapped in the respect and honor due a giant of a man.

His civic contributions were numerous, his loyalty to his God and church monumental. He was a man of character and wisdom, and he possessed a legendary sense of humor. While I admired and respected him greatly for his other traits, it was his sharp wit and humorous outlook on life that I wish to remember. If there really has ever been a man who could be characterized as a real bonafide American, I feel that Marshall Chapman would fill the bill.

The two of us shared an affinity for good apples, especially North Carolina apples. On many occasions I delivered apples to him after returning home from North Carolina, and he in turn reciprocated.

On one occasion shortly before his death, I met him on a downtown street and told him that I had just returned from North Carolina that day and had some apples for him at my house.

"Well, they're not doing me any good there," he said in mock anger. "Go and get them!"

I did just that and enjoyed watching him chuckle in pretended embarrassment as I placed a large bag on his kitchen table.

At one time Mr. Chapman was an avid, dedicated golfer. One Sunday afternoon in the early 1980s after we had enjoyed the Sunday noon buffet at the Dublin Country Club, I invited him to join me for a ride around the golf course. It was a beautiful day, and he accepted. With his ever-present walking stick in hand, he climbed into my golf cart.

As we rolled along, he made repeated comments about his golfing days and then, suddenly, as we rode down the 14th fairway toward the green, he motioned with his walking stick toward the wooded area on our right.

"Drive up there for a minute," he ordered.

No sooner had we made the move and found ourselves surrounded by trees and bushes, than I heard him say, "Now, that's better. This is much more familiar territory to me than the fairway."

On another occasion in 1980, when he was a spry eighty-seven years old, during an economic slump he was asked by a good friend, Bush Perry, what he thought about the economy and how the future looked to him. He didn't hesitate and replied, "Well, Bush, the future looks all right to me. In fact, just this morning I bought a new car battery that has a four-year warranty."

On still another occasion, a bitter cold day in January, I was present for a lunch table discussion that included Mr. Chapman and several of his good friends at a local restaurant. The conversation centered around the cold weather and automobiles, particularly concern over frozen radiators and cracked motor blocks.

The subject of freeze plugs came up, and Mr. Chapman expressed a noticeable interest in them, along with an admitted ignorance regarding their purpose. He then proceeded to direct several questions to his friend Cordy Green, who was more familiar with automobiles.

"What do freeze plugs do, Cordy? Do you reckon my car has freeze plugs? Should I have my freeze plug checked?"

Green explained the function of freeze plugs—to expand and prevent the motor block from cracking. He also assured Mr. Chapman that there were indeed freeze plugs in his car's motor and reminded him that they should be checked periodically.

"I don't doubt your word, Cordy, but I've owned cars since 1915 and today is the first time I ever heard about freeze plugs," he answered.

Some twenty minutes later, after leaving the restaurant, Bush Perry and I pulled into Dave Brinson's Chevron station for gasoline. Mr. Chapman pulled in a short time later, spoke with Dave Brinson, and asked him if he would please check his freeze plug. He then spotted Bush and me and, no doubt recalling the earlier conversation, said to Brinson, "I make it a point to have my freeze plug checked every sixty-five years, Dave."

Marshall Chapman was an original. He was wise, witty, and a good friend. He left Dublin, Georgia, a much better community than he found when he arrived in 1909.

Why Live in the South? The People!

If I were reading instead of writing this, I seriously doubt that I would believe it.

I have been asked many times in my travels around the country why I chose to live in Middle Georgia when, being retired and single, I could have lived anywhere.

"The people" is my standard reply.

Here's a concrete example:

On February 26, 1990, I started out to drive to Sylvania, Georgia, from my home in Dublin, Georgia, a distance of ninety-two miles. I left at 4:00 P.M. to get there in time for a 7:00 P.M. speech to the Sylvania Lions Club Ladies Night Banquet. At 5:20 P.M. I passed the Metter, Georgia, exit on Interstate 16. Six miles later my car suddenly went bananas. As the motor burped and gagged like it had overdosed on liver, I pulled off in the emergency lane. The car died an unceremonious death at 5:37 P.M., right next to mile post 108.

I started walking. To Sylvania? No, to look for any sign of life— maybe a light.

I walked about a mile to the Pulaski-Excelsior exit where I saw Franklin's Truck Stop, a welcome water hole in the I-26 oasis.

There were eight or ten tractor-trailer rigs in the giant parking lot. I stepped inside the truckers' store all decked out in my white slacks, navy blue blazer, blue oxford cloth button-down shirt, navy and red-striped tie, and black tassel loafers. Several truckers were seated around, talking trucker talk. I was as conspicuous as a peacock in a pigeon roost.

I approached the man at the cash register, learned that he was the owner, and explained my problem. I asked if there was a mechanic on the premises. Negative.

"Let's go look at your car," he said without hesitation.

We got in his Ford pickup, and he drove to my car. He took a quick look and checked it out. No pulse, no heartbeat. I locked it, and he drove back to the truck stop, pulled his pickup alongside a gas pump, and filled the tank with regular unleaded.

"What time did you say you got to be in Sylvania?" he asked.

"Seven," I answered, glancing at my watch. It was 6:10 P.M.

"Just take my pickup and go ahead," he said. "I jus' bought it this mornin', so it oughta run all right. I'll get your car pulled in. Jus' stop here on your way back after the meetin' an' call me. I'll be at home, in Metter."

I didn't know Grady Franklin from Adam and said to him in a tone not intended to be really convicing, "I can't do that, Mr. Franklin. I . . ."

"Well, you can't walk to Sylvania and get there by 7 o'clock. It's forty-two miles," he reasoned. "Now take my truck and go on. I'll figure out somethin' by the time you get back."

I did just that. I took his truck and went on, arriving at the Sylvania Civic Center at 6:57 P.M. The program chairman, Bill Tyre, met me at the door.

"Have a nice ride over?" he asked.

"Interesting, Bill. Very interesting," I answered, letting it go at that.

I ate, gave the speech, and drove back to Franklin's Truck Stop. When I arrived at 10:30 P.M., I called Grady Franklin at his home in Metter, eight miles away. He told me that he had my car towed to Franklin Chevrolet, and they would check it out the next morning.

"Now then, how're you gonna' get to Dublin?" he asked.

"Well, I don't know," I answered, "but I have to be in Macon at noon tomorrow to speak at the Eighth District Star Student Awards Luncheon."

"Take my truck," he said. "Bring it back when you can. In the meantime, I'll check on your car at the Chevrolet place."

Again—without hesitation—I accepted his offer. I drove home, spent the night, drove to Macon the next morning, made my speech, drove back to Metter and returned his truck. My car was fixed.

I thanked Grady Franklin repeatedly.

"Aw, glad to help out," he said. "By the way, you ain't the same Bo Whaley who writes Redneck books are you?"

"Well, yes I am. I have to admit it," I said.

"I've got all your books in my truck stop. They sell real good."

"Thanks, I appreciate that."

"Me and my wife's got all your books at home," he said. "I was wonderin' if you'd mind autographing them for us?"

"Certainly, I'll be more than glad to," I assured him.

And I did.

Another thing—I had two hundred more in the trunk of my car that he could have had for the asking.

Middle Georgia hospitality. People helping people. That's why I live in Middle Georgia.

There's No Place Like the South

It's great to live in the South. I mean, I'm talking real South. Any Zip Code north of the Mason/Dixon Line won't get it.

I served my sentence in Detroit, New York, and Newark—thirteen years without parole—and learned one thing above all else: the best days there are Fridays when the natives scatter like flies to warmer, southern environs. The worst days? Sundays, when they are forced to return to mass hysteria and wait for Friday.

I learned shortly after my arrival in Detroit, and subsequently New York and Newark, that people don't even wave at each other up there. I grew up in South Georgia waving at folks who waved back. Wave in northern cities, and people think you're soliciting. I think you could actually get arrested for waving on Woodward Avenue in Detroit, Broadway in New York, or Frelinghuysen Avenue in Newark.

Living in the South gives you license to wave. Friendly waves to farmers on tractors, people in pickup trucks, school bus drivers and the kids peering out the back window, folks sitting on porches, and highway work crews are considered neighborly gestures. Most wave back. If they don't, I classify them as snooty, just passing through, or moved south recently from someplace north of Nashville.

I wave in town and country, particularly at drivers who permit me to back out of a parking space in heavy traffic on a busy downtown street, or in busy and maniacal parking lots like at the post office or the courthouse.

Also, I wave at every law enforcement officer as if to say, "Hi! I'm okay, you're okay—and I have a valid driver's license and insurance card."

There is one accepted signal of recognition down in God's country, the lifting of one finger (*always* the forefinger) from the steering wheel in a respectful salute. Use the wrong finger, and you could be in a heap o' trouble, boy. All-night fights have been ignited by such a digital error.

Of course, in heavy, congested traffic up north drivers employ the digital salute to fellow motorists, but they use a different finger.

Waving is a sign language, a way of saying hello from a distance. It is a universal sign language. One legendary waver was the

"Waving Girl" in Savannah. A statue of the unknown miss overlooks the Savannah River where she stood for years and waved at seamen on passing ships from all over the world as they entered or left the port of Savannah.

There are, of course, certain rules about waving. Here are but a few:

• If you are on foot, say looking over your garden, the responsibility for waving at passing vehicles is squarely on your shoulders.

• If you are burdened down with an armload of corn, tomatoes, or okra, it will suffice to jerk your head up and down—*but* never side to side. That, friend, is a no-no and tantamount to saying, "I don't have the time to be bothered with you."

• It is strictly up to you to decide if you are going to wave when you see or hear an approaching vehicle. If for some reason you don't feel like waving or recognize the vehicle as that of a snob you don't like, just lower your head and study the pea vines, cucumber plants, or squash. However, if you look up and make eye contact, then you are duty bound to wave, even if it hurts to do so. Your mama wouldn't like it if you didn't wave.

• If you are shuffling back and forth on a country road, it is not necessary to wave at the same person more than once a day. Neither is it expected that you will do so. Once a day is enough. People will think nothing of it because they abide by the same rule.

• Some folks have other things to do besides waving all day long, but not porch sitters who wave at log trucks, the mailman, kids on bicycles, deputy sheriffs, and maybe a school bus late in the afternoon or early in the morning. Also, people who live near railroad tracks wouldn't think of not waving at the engineer. And you can bet he'll always wave back. Subways? No. Railroads? Yes. It's a railroad tradition of long standing.

• Horn-honking in lieu of waving in the country is out. Only a city slicker honks at anybody in the country.

• Heavy rainstorms, hailstorms, tornadoes, strong wind, or anything causing property damage calls for waving at anyone who is out surveying the scene. A wave is a kind of "All clear. The damage has been done, it's over, and we survived." It is really an acknowledgment of survival.

• I realize that everybody is not into waving, so if you don't want to wave, don't. If you're in a vehicle and wish to refrain, that's a good time to tune the radio. If caught on foot, squat and tie your shoe. If caught in the middle of sending out an unintentional wave with your hand shoulder high, simply scratch your ear, slick your hair down, or feign a yawn. It will all pass in a few seconds.

I know lots of people in Atlanta who don't wave. Waves were in vogue there a few years ago at Braves games, but in recent years there haven't been enough people in the stands to get one started.

Good Ole Boys Are Going Out of Style

As a Southerner bred and born, I can tell that good ole boys are no longer in style. A southern boy is what the yuppies refer to as passé, a French word meaning something close to being as necessary as a wedding ring to a tomcat.

I left my beloved Southland in 1954 and for the next twenty years docked in Detroit, New York, New Jersey, Wisconsin, and Minnesota. I discovered many truths, like these:

One: People from the Midwest treat language like golf; they pretty much play it as it lays. Words are just a form of communication, and they can't understand that in the South language is an art form. Midwesterners seldom say more than "have a seat." They don't know the joy of saying "put your butt down and set a spell."

The southern language is to English what French is to the other languages of the world—the language of love. I discovered many years ago that a southern belle from Middle Georgia could make my blood boil by just reading the telephone book with her southern accent. God let it forever be preserved! And a true southern belle can make a vowel sound last longer than a crooked election or a root canal.

Two: People in the Midwest and East, think all Southerners sound alike, no matter what part of Dixie they're from. They also think we have a lot of cousins marrying cousins down here.

When I was working out of Newark, my partner for several years was Ray Davis from East Tennessee. If we heard it once, we heard it a thousand times, "Well, you're both from the South. Why don't you talk alike?" They would never believe that even a person living in, say, Blairsville would have a rough time understanding one living in, say, Alma. The accents are as different as Russian and Swahili.

Three: The same Midwesterners and Easterners think that anyone with a southern drawl has the mentality of a stump. I don't blame them. I blame it on Hollywood. Think about it. When was the last time someone with a southern drawl was portrayed as intelligent in a movie or television show? Gomer Pyle? Goober? Junior Samples? Lulu? "Green Acres"? "Designing Women"? All were cast as main characters and country rubes. The worst, of course, was "Dukes of Hazzard."

The television show "Newhart" had three characters named Larry, Daryl, and Daryl. Only Larry spoke. Larry was supposed to be from Vermont, but to make him sound stupid what sort of accent did they assign him? The Tennessee riverbelt. Why else would anyone from Vermont have a Tennessee accent?

Go north and see what happens. As soon as people above the Mason–Dixon line hear that southern drawl, they treat you like you're from Mozambique, Guatemala, Sweden, Miami, or some other foreign country. They automatically begin to talk very slowly, very loudly, and they make many hand gestures. I tried very patiently to explain to them that I talk slow but I'm not stupid, and that usually worked unless they had met a Southerner who wasn't very intelligent. Then they were totally convinced that everyone in the South had the IQ of a rock.

Four: People who ain't "frum 'round heah" have no idea what makes up the "true" South. But every true Southerner knows that the South is made up of only the states of North and South Carolina, Tennessee, Alabama, Mississippi, Louisiana, southern Kentucky, eastern Arkansas, and Georgia (after eliminating Atlanta and parts of Gwinett County).

Do they think Florida, Virginia, and Texas are included in the true South. No way!

Texas is part of the West, and Florida is one big tourist stop filled with Canadians with funny money, Japanese with cameras, and New Yorkers with poodles. Virginia is nothing more than a haven for Washington lobbyists and politicians, and the final resting place for dead heroes.

Hard to Get a Straight Answer These Days

Straight answers are getting harder to come by these days. Watch a political show like "Meet the Press," "Face the Nation," or "Crossfire." Listen to a press conference. Read a government news release. Ask somebody to explain Medicare or Quality Basic Education. Read an insurance policy. Look at a prescription. If you can comprehend what you hear and read, you are indeed the exception.

There is one place where, as a general rule, you can get a straight answer—the country store. A good example is the man from Boston who was on his way to Florida and stopped at a country store in South Georgia for a Coke and a package of crackers.

Sitting on a Coca-Cola crate in front of the store was an old gentleman reading a newspaper. As the Bostonian approached him, he asked, "Have you lived around here all your life, old timer?"

"Nope. Not yet, I ain't," the old man replied without looking up from the newspaper.

That, friend, is a straight answer.

My grandpa owned a country store in Hancock County, halfway between Sparta and Crawfordville, for years, and I spent many happy hours there as a boy.

Grandpa loved to tell the story about his good friend Robert Barksdale, a railroad man, and his standard reply to anyone who asked him if he knew what time it was. With a straight face Robert would take his railroad watch from his watch pocket, look as it, return it to the pocket, and say, "Yep."

I thought about these two stories after I had stopped in a country store a few weeks ago on my way to Waycross. It was one of those stores that is fast fading, sadly, from the American scene. It's owned by the man who runs it, and he lives in a little house behind it. Neither has felt the touch of a paintbrush, at least since World War II. A couple of nondescript dogs laze around in front, and there is no self-service gas pump. The owner does the pumping and everything else that has to be done at the store. His cash register is mechanical, and he gives credit to the locals, writing the amount in a well-worn writing tablet.

His wife cooks dinner (lunch) for him, and the sign on the front door says, "Closed For Lunch, 12 to 1." It is my guess that he squeezes a short nap in there somewhere. And there are Cokes in six-ounce bottles in the cooler and a checker-board on the counter at one end and a picture of a young man in a navy uniform on the wall.

I had a Coke, stretched my legs, and rested for a little while on a bench out front. The owner, an older man wearing overalls and a hat, came out and joined me.

We talked in generalities for a few minutes before a car occupied by a young boy and girl pulled up and stopped. Both appeared to be about eighteen.

The girl was driving, and the boy got out and went inside the store. The owner followed him, and I followed both of them to return my six-ounce Coke bottle. Like I said, it was a country store.

I saw the boy buy cigarette papers, a box of matches, and two candy bars. I looked at his eyes and saw a far away look in them like he hadn't slept in a week. He was in a daze, the kind of look that pot smokers have. An earring dangled from his pierced left ear, and his long, stringy hair hung down below his shoulders.

I walked outside with the store owner, and we watched them leave in a hurry.

"What did you think of him?" he asked.

"Well, I don't know," I said. "What do you think?"

"I figure he ain't worth killing," he said, then turned and walked back inside.

Another straight answer.

Part 3

If It Ain't Broke —Don't Fix It!

Some people have the ability to repair, rebuild, or remodel anything from diesel engines to television sets. Me? I go bananas just trying to put a new ribbon in my typewriter, removing and replacing my automobile ash tray, or making vain attempts to hang wall pictures.

I may well be the only man in Georgia with a forty-five-degree ocean in his living room and bird dogs in the den with all four feet pointed toward the ceiling.

A handyman I ain't.

Calling Mr. Goodwrench

I REALIZED THAT I needed a trailer hitch on my car so I proceeded to inquire about having one put on. "No problem," I was told. "I can put that little baby on there for seventy-five dollars." I decided to have it done. However, in discussing the matter with my friend Ben Canady, on leave from the United States Army in Germany, he assured me that he could do the job for twenty-five dollars. I agreed, and he did it in just about an hour.

I was so pleased at my savings on the trailer hitch that I really went into a thrift syndrome. Overnight I became a one-man fix-'em-up gang, much to my regret.

First, I decided that if Ben could do such a good job on the trailer hitch and save me fifty dollars in the process, why not me? So I gave it a try.

I don't think my car even needed an oil change or new spark plugs but, with my new-found enthusiasm and new worlds to conquer in the automobile repair field, I would have done it if I had just rolled a new Seville off the showroom floor. Also, I would have done it with all the confidence in the world that when I finished, I would be as neat and well groomed as Mr. Goodwrench. So I made preparations to perform surgery on my 1975 Oldsmobile.

First, I bought five quarts of oil and a filter. I couldn't wait to get to the parts store and get the plugs, eight of 'em. Then I hurried home to my back yard operating room to begin.

I found out right quick that you don't just reach under and loosen the bolt and expect the oil to wait for you to move before it starts spurting out in the waiting pan. Nope. It jumps out like a Texas gusher, unexpectedly. Also, there just ain't enough room to jerk your head out of the way when it starts. Instead of a surgeon, I was quickly transformed into an eye, ear, nose, and throat man, because that's exactly the area that was covered with black, dirty oil—my eyes, ears, nose, and throat.

Second, I reached for the oil filter. No problem here, I thought, just twist the old one off and twist the new one on. Right? Wrong! You can't do that without a filter tool. I've seen Mr. Goodwrench do it many times, but he has a filter tool. Into the bathroom, wash up, and head back to the parts store to buy a filter tool. Is the picture getting clearer?

With the filter tool firmly in hand I just took that old filter off before you could say "handyman."

"Nothing to this," I said to myself. However, Murphy's Law began to raise its ugly head when I tried, unsuccessfully, to fit a Volkswagen filter into a hole specifically designed for a 1975 Oldsmobile. Was I defeated? Heck, no! I did something that would make Mr. Goodwrench turn over in his grease pit! I simply put the old filter back on, as every good, dedicated do-it-yourself amateur would do.

Now, it was time to put in the new oil. Very simple, right? Wrong! You see, to make it easier, I had bought one of those seventy-nine-cent thingamajigs that allow you to perforate the oil can and thereby have a spout for easy pouring. The only problem was it leaked something awful!

So, after losing one of my five quarts all over the motor and the grass, I decided that four would be sufficient. Without the spout, I succeeded in pouring those four quarts of oil in without spilling a drop. I didn't spill a drop on the motor, that is, but all I really did was run it through. Here is why. Let me give all you would-be self-oil-changers a simple warning: *Always replace the oil drain plug before pouring in the new oil!*

I now have the blackest grass in Laurens County.

Well, there are times when we just have to accept our limitations. I closed the hood, drove real slow to my friend Tommy Daniel's Shell station, and explained to him that I was a real busy man and needed my oil changed as well as my filter and plugs. I didn't say, "spark plugs"; only an amateur would say that. I just said "plugs." He wasn't impressed.

"I could do it myself, in just a few minutes, you know, if I had the time," I told him nonchalantly.

"Right, Bo. I know." I have the feeling that he does. That's what bothers me.

The only thing I really accomplished was to blow the fifty dollars Ben saved me on the trailer hitch. I wonder if Mr. Goodwrench would like to buy an oil filter tool real cheap, and does anybody need a Volkswagen oil filter?

All Plumbers Are Underpaid

How much do plumbers charge per hour? $12? $18? $75? $375? It makes no difference. I'm convinced they are grossly underpaid!

Last Saturday made a believer out of me. From this day forward you'll not read a derogatory word about plumbers written by me.

It happened this way.

Every year or two I go absolutely crazy and tackle my storage house. Nineteen eighty-six is my year. I don't know why I thought this year would be any different. I do the same thing every time I take a smart (or dumb) pill and turn on to the storage house.

First, the boxes come out, the same boxes I've hauled all over the United States. Then, I take everything out of them and spread the conglomeration on the lawn. I make a solemn vow that *this* year I'm gonna' throw at least half the junk away. After all, who needs a 1957 calendar, a gear shift knob for a 1962 TR-3, a 1949 identification bracelet engraved "Walker W. Whaley," seven corroded keys that fit nothing in Dublin, three locks with no keys, plus a combination lock with the combination long ago lost and forgotten?

This is not to mention such collectibles as a book on the art of hula-hooping; a jacket the Salvation Army has rejected twice; a pair of trousers I couldn't get into with the help of a sardine packer; a faded and blurred certificate of appreciation from the Pontiac, Michigan, Police Department, twelve pencils; an out-of-date wedding ring; a National Bank of Detroit key chain; a broken seven-iron; baseball glove, vintage 1952; an ash tray from Canada; a broken air rifle that I bought from Hansley Horne at Laurens Hardware in the early '50s; several baseballs; assorted broken sunglasses and cigarette lighters.

I took a look and eyed the boxes yet to be emptied. To heck with it! It was time for a break.

On my way to town, astride my trusty Harley Davidson, for a cup of coffee, I detoured and rode by a friend's house. You never know, maybe she had the coffee pot on.

"Anybody home? How's it going?"

"I'm back here," the voice rang out from the remote regions of her daughter's room, "and I'm beat and disgusted."

"What's the matter?"

"Oh, I've been working for hours trying to fix the drain under the lavatory in this bathroom. Impossible," she said wearily.

It was at this point that I made my mistake.

"Here, let me have that pipe wrench. I'll fix that booger in no time flat."

She handed me the wrench but flashed a knowing grin based on her knowledge of my past performances in changing oil, repairing(?) lawn mowers, hunting lost hubcaps, and hanging wallpaper.

Not wanting to see a grown man cry, she moved on to the kitchen. I moved under the lavatory just far enough so that there were two Head and Shoulders under there, as well as more shampoo, hair rollers, rinse, make-up, eye stuff—more creams and junk than in all the drug stores in Atlantic City during Miss America week. No wonder Mary Kay and Merle Norman are billionaires!

I twisted and turned for forty-five minutes trying to connect the cotton pickin' drain pipe. No luck. Then I made a brilliant observation, one that a plumber would have made before turning over the Lilt and getting his sweater tangled up in the hair rollers. (Ever fight eighteen rabid, raging porcupines while imitating a pretzel under a bathroom lavatory?)

There were no threads on the end of the pipe I was trying to connect. Stupid! Just plain stupid! I should have noticed that before I turned the waste basket over with my foot.

I marched past the kitchen and out the front door. She was sitting at the bar drinking MY coffee with a friend.

"Got it fixed?" she called out as I bolted out the door.

"I don't wanna' talk about it!" I called back to her and straddled my motorcycle, stuffing the piece of amputated pipe under my windbreaker.

Once downtown, I marched into the hardware store and cornered Don Jones. He listened patiently as I explained the bathroom lavatory situation in minute detail, holding the pipe in front of me like a wounded snake.

"Simple. You need a new section. This one's got no threads," Don told me.

I pretended not to hear. I merely took the new section, climbed back on my motorcycle, and headed back to the john.

Did I fix the leaky drain by connecting the pieces? Come on now, you know the answer to that.

Back on the motorcycle and back to the hardware store. Another session with Don Jones. His answer?

"You need the whole section," he said.

"Let me have it," I said, without hesitation. At that point I would have signed for a new bathroom.

"Does the main drain pipe you're connecting to go through the floor or the wall?" he asked with a straight face.

Man, I don't know about the pipe but I was ready to go through the ceiling.

"Through the floor," I said with all the nonchalance of a master plumber.

(For the information of all you nonhandymen, it *does* make a difference. Through the wall, and that son-of-a-gun makes more turns than the street in front of the Carnegie Library. I was to learn this little-known fact soon.)

Same song, second verse. Back on the motorcycle and back to the john with a drain pipe sticking out of my windbreaker and above my head. I could have sworn I heard a guy comment as I turned on Gaines Street, "Man, I ain't never seen no diesel Harley Davidson before!"

They were on their second cup when I walked in. I marched right by them. The porcupines were crouched and waiting.

Does that main drain pipe go through the floor? Of course not! It goes straight down into the clump of porcupines, then makes a ninety-degree turn through the shampoo and rinse bottles before disappearing through the *wall* and continues on out Claxton Dairy Road to Dudley as far as I know. I may never know. Only her plumber knows for sure because I stormed to the kitchen and told her to do just that. Call her plumber.

No matter what he charges he'll be underpaid as far as I'm concerned. He'd just better watch out for those darned porcupines. They'll attack at the drop of a pipe wrench.

I would have finished the job myself but I just didn't have the nerve to face Don Jones a third time in one afternoon.

What happened to the stuff I took out of the storage house? The same thing that happens every two years. I put it all back inside where it'll stay until another year. One difference. Now there is a pipe wrench added to the collection and I obviously have no more use for that than I do for the TR-3 gear shift knob, corroded keys, and broken sunglasses.

All together, now, let's hear it for the plumbers. Ready?"

"Two, four, six, eight! Who do we appreciate? The plumbers!"

Eating While Driving Should Be Illegal

Drinking while driving is against the law, right? The law badly needs amending to add eating. Amend the law and I'll be the first to plead guilty.

I have this continuing fear that when I go it'll be in a bad auto accident while I'm trying to open a can of Vienna sausage, nursing a stupid hot dog bun that keeps dripping mustard and ketchup, or struggling with a pop-top on a can of Coca Cola.

Some drivers are just plain dumb; put me on the list. I can't drive without eating. No matter where I'm going, I don't get a mile out of the Dublin city limits before I start looking for one of those lighted signs in front of a convenience store. You've seen 'em: Jack's Mini-Mart—Col Be r To Go—Mi k $2.19 Gal.—Fish Bates Fo Sail. Go Dawgs!

The sign always has thirteen letters missing and eighteen dead light bulbs. The guy behind the cash register always wears a cap and smokes a cigar. A supply of boiled peanuts and hoop cheese dominates the counter. It's hard for me to pass up either.

A normal purchase for me is a can of Coke, a can of Vienna sausage, two packages of saltines, potato chips, and a cinnamon roll for desert.

On good days, I might make it a mile before spilling the Coke, but I will spill it. You can wager the egg money on that. Heck, I may have the only car in America that has a burping floorboard.

If you are dead set on eating and driving, it's important to learn how to set the car table.

The Coke goes between your legs. Mistake number one.

Open the Vienna sausage *before* pulling away from the store even though the store owner will probably frown and curse when you dump the juice on the ground next to the broken ice machine. Don't sweat it, it's a heck of a lot better than trying to pout it out the window going sixty miles per hour and winding up with Vienna sausage juice on your left shoulder and in your left ear.

Once opened, the Vienna sausage go on the dash.

The hoop cheese, once unwrapped, goes on the seat.

The saltines go next to the cheese.

The boiled peanuts go next to the Vienna sausage.

The potato chips join the Coke. Mistake number two.

The cinnamon roll? Leave it in the bag which is located directly in the firing line of the heater fan. The white stuff on top gets gooey quicker that way so when you reach for it later it feels like you've grabbed hold of a busted container of Elmer's glue.

There are many things that I fail to understand about animals, such as a deer that will stand still as a car with a dead battery and watch you approach for two miles until you are within thirty yards. You know what happens, don't you? He decides that he simply has to cross to the other side of Georgia 257.

While Bambi usually makes it across 257, he sure as heck upsets your car table as you swerve to miss him.

Vienna sausages slide across the dash and wind up in the windshield defroster vent and what juice remains drips into the glove compartment. The boiled peanuts sound like hail as they pepper the windshield and fall to the floorboard.

When you finally regain control of the car, you experience the strange sensation between your legs that (1) the dam at Lake Sinclair has busted, or (2) you are holding your eight-month-old grandchild, the one with the kidney problem.

And how in the devil can the Coca Cola company squeeze two-and-a-half gallons of Coke into a twelve-ounce can?

The potato chips are as soggy as a tomato sandwich in August, victims of the Coke flood.

What happened to the cheese! It's over there somewhere between the front seat and the right front door. Ty Cobb never made a better slide.

The only thing to do is discount your loss and mentally kick yourself.

You look for another sign that will inevitably loom before you: Sp cial—Burg r, fr fri s an la ge Coke—.99 cent—Go Dawgs!

You pull in, park, and walk in like Wilt Chamberlain trying to crouch under a limbo stick in a vain attempt to hide the effects of the broken dam or grandchild calamity. After all, it's better to be looked upon as a deformed limbo rock dancer than to make any attempt at an explanation.

"Gimme' the special," you call up to the waitress behind the four-foot counter.

"To take out?" she asks.

"No thanks, I'll just spill it here."

She hands you a number after you hand her $1.03. Then you wait.

"Who gets 194?" she finally yells.

"The crippled guy over there by the jukebox," somebody replies.

Twelve sympathizers stare at you. You smile humbly. They're all wondering the same thing: What happened to him?

You say nothing. After all, how do you explain that you broke the law, eating and driving, and Lake Sinclair or your eight-month-old-grandchild flooded your lap?

Progress Breeds Complications

Do you ever find yourself thinking back to the way things used to be? I'm guilty. I do it all the time. Oh, I'm not saying that I would like to see us revert back to what we sometimes refer to as "the good old days," but it seems to me that progress does breed complications. Here are a few "for instances" that come to mind:

• Medicine bottles. Do you remember what you had to do in the middle of the night a few years back if you woke up with a headache? You simply stumbled to the medicine chest or reached over to the nightstand and picked up a bottle of aspirin, took a couple, and went back to sleep without ever even turning a light on. No more.

First, you have to determine just what kind of headache you have. Is it an Excedrin headache, a sinus headache, or just what? Do you want to have a race between a Bufferin and an aspirin? After you make your diagnosis, you then have to become an expert safecracker in order to get the cotton pickin' top off the bottle you selected. It's hard enough to do it in the daylight and now you sit there in the dark and try to line up the arrow with the opening for some relief. I am convinced that the manufacturers of the "Bayer's New Exclusive Child-Guard Slide Pack" that houses your instant relief are in cahoots with the manufacturers of Band-Aids and nail clippers, as I have never opened one yet without cutting a finger or breaking a fingernail.

They don't have to worry at all about children opening them, although I feel certain that the faculty at M.I.T. would experience great difficulty in successfully manipulating the contraption.

• Coffee creamers. Remember way back when you used to go in and sit down in your favorite coffee spot and just simply pour the desired amount of cream into your coffee from a cream pitcher (or a Carnation milk can)? No more!

Progress has moved full force into the area of coffee creamers. Now you sit down and the waitress brings your coffee with that little triangular-shaped object sitting on your saucer just waiting for your nimble little fingers to manipulate it. Oh, the directions are printed thereon plain and clear, but nobody, including yours truly, ever reads them.

My established routine is to pick the thing up and attempt to open it real easy with one hand while holding it securely with the other. Completely wrong! I either squirt myself in the nose, the fellow sitting on my left in the right ear, the fellow sitting on my right in the left ear, or the fellow sitting across from me on the tie! I do it so much that I have been tempted to have some cards printed that read Very Sorry to pass out after I squirt them or Watch Out before I attempt to open the monstrosity. Heck, on a good day, I have been known to squirt a lady in the back of the neck two tables away!

Progress? I guess we have made some, but those little triangular doodads ain't part of it! Just give me a good ol' cream pitcher any day.

• Cracker boxes. I defy you to follow the directions and open one but not tear the top of the box in half. Oh, I know what it says, and I've tried it o'er and o'er again only to wind up with a piece of the lid in my hand and a cracker box with ants in it a few days later. It all sounds very simple. "Tear along dotted line and tuck flap into slot." Baloney! It won't work. The first couple of inches go as straight as an arrow and then the darn thing veers off the track like a drunken railroad engineer! Then, I have a choice. I can go ahead and eat all the crackers or know that the next time I take some out they are going to be stale.

Progress? Maybe, but just give me the old box that I grew up with that I took my mother's butcher knife and partially cut open one end.

• Potato chips. This is one of my favorite peeves. How many of you can honestly do what it says on the package: Tear Here?

I don't know what they make those containers out of, but I'm convinced that the Army could ship a tank in one from Fort Stewart to Germany and it would arrive intact.

I have solved this one. Yep, I beat ol' man progress! I eat Pringles so all I have to do is open the can. (Have you tried to open a package of sliced cheese? Back to mama's butcher knife for me!)

• Toilet tissue. I guess all our modern and pretty colored packages of Scott Tissue, Charmin, Delsey, and the others do represent progress when we compare them to the old Sears-Roebuck catalog. However, I think I can best describe my frustrations with toilet tissue by relating a story that really says it better than I can.

It seems that a leading manufacturer of airplanes was experiencing an awful lot of difficulty with its newest jet model. Every time it was test flown, the right wing would come off flush with the fuselage. After some fifteen such unsuccessful tests, all the company's best designers were huddled around a table in the assembly area trying to solve the problem of that right wing coming off. An elderly man in overalls walked by and leaned in to see what was being discussed. After watching and listening for a few seconds, he spoke up.

"Why don't you perforate it?" he announced matter-of-factly.

All the designers turned to look at the old gentleman and the chief designer spoke to him.

"Who are you? What do you mean perforate it?"

"My name's Howard. I'm the janitor. Jus' thought if you was still havin' trouble with that right wing comin' off, you might perforate it."

"Well, what good would that do?" the chief designer asked very sarcastically.

"Well, I been puttin' toilet tissue in the restrooms here for the past thirty years and I ain't never seen a roll yet that tears where it's perforated!"

Changes Are Just Hard to Accept

I have already done it twice this morning and will, no doubt, repeat the error numerous times over the next few weeks. Has it happened to you yet? What am I talking about? Well, just take a look at this and see if it looks familiar to you. Have you written any letters or checks where the dateline looks like this:

Dublin, Georgia

January 3, ~~1978~~ 1979

If you have, don't feel too bad about it. It is such a universal error that Norman Rockwell made it the subject of one of his famous *Saturday Evening Post* covers many years ago. I won't be able to get my days straightened out until Monday and it may be well into February before I can write 1986 without hesitating. Man! I just hope the government doesn't decide one of these years to change the time and the year at the same time! No way I would ever get that straight! I can just see me walking into church

some January Saturday morning at 10:00 A.M. and not finding a
soul there, but I was there Christmas Day, alone, and it was sort
of comforting.

I guess we just get so used to a daily routine that any change
from it kind of throws us off track. For instance, just suppose you
came in from a fishing or hunting trip in the early morning hours,
say about 2:00 A.M. Naturally you wouldn't want to wake the family at such an hour so you decide to maneuver quietly through the
living room and up the stairs to your bedroom. However, you are
completely unaware that the Mrs. has rearranged every stick of
furniture in the living room. You know as well as I do what would
happen, don't you? Lamps and chairs would go one way while
you fell over the coffee table like a wounded elephant! Yes, it's just
hard to accept changes.

For instance, I recall that in 1973, my son had a nice little compact car. He had received it for graduation from high school in
1970, in Swainsboro, and it served him well during his tenure at
Middle Georgia College for the next two years.

Well, he was to take a trip to Nashville, Tennessee, and it was
decided that he would use my car since it was larger and had more
truck space. So he left his little gem with me.

Not long after he left it became necessary for me to make an
emergency trip from Lyons to Sparta, a drive of approximately
one hundred miles. The telephone call came late at night and I
was on my way, in his midget and in the rain. Have you driven a
strange car lately? It can be an experience.

First, after pulling out of my mother's driveway, I reached for
what I thought was the windshield wiper switch (it would have
been on my car) and succeeded in pulling the knob off the radio
volume control, dropping it on the floor. I tried another knob and
the windshield wipers lay as still as a petrified tree. No wonder, I
had turned on the heater this time. So I pulled off the road to take
a knob inventory, with no flashlight but with the aid of a cigarette
lighter. I found the windshield wiper switch and thought I was in
good shape as I pulled back on to U.S. Highway 1 for my journey
northward. But, in my little inspection, I had neglected to locate
the dimmer switch.

Now every car I have ever owned since 1946 has had the cotton
pickin' dimmer switch located under my left foot. How about
yours? Not so on my son's little foreign beauty! I nearly pushed a

hole in the floorboard just to the left of the clutch pedal trying to dim the lights as I repeatedly met everything from eighteen-wheelers and buses to motorcycles, all blinking at me like a Navy signal light operator flashing the Morse Code.

The rain continued to fall, but I felt like sticking my head out the window and yelling to each blinker as he passed (and cursed) me, "I'm trying, buddy! I just can't find the dimmer switch on this little !$⁹!!"

It was off the road again for another inspection on the outskirts of Oak Park, where with all the fluid burned out of my Zippo, I had to make this one in braille. I think I must have pulled, grabbed, and twisted everything on and under the dash and still those oncoming lights glared like giant searchlights. No dimmer switch!

I pictured my son cruising up the expressway between Atlanta and Chattanooga, listening to his favorite tape, with the cruise control set and the automatic dimmer switch working perfectly!

Then I saw what appeared to be a service station up ahead in Oak Park. I drove straight to it and pulled in. The old gentleman seated behind the counter inside looked at me like he thought I was crazy when I asked if anyone there could help me locate the dimmer switch on my car. But before he could have me mentally committed, a young boy, about seventeen, rescued me:

"I think it's on the turn signal lever, mister."

He was right! I could have kissed him—and would have, but you just don't do that in Oak Park!

Yep, sometimes changes are just hard to accept. The two dollar bill is ample evidence of that, isn't it?

At any rate, I sincerely hope that 1979 will be a great one for you and that peace and prosperity will come to the world. It will be what we make it, that's for sure. And, as is true of every new year, it will bring changes, many changes. But, we will accept them. We always have. Just as we did in 1978, we will adjust in 1979.

Would-be Handyman Is All Thumbs

Some days things just don't go right. Take last Saturday, and I wish you had, because it was a bummer for me.

First off, it was a beautiful day and that turned me on. I decided to do something constructive; you know, fix something, just get hammer and nails and start pounding. Ever had the feeling? If not, and you get it, just walk around the block, buy a newspaper or go shoot a couple of games of eight-ball and it'll go away. I well remember the last time it hit me. I broke a hammer, busted a water pipe, got a blister on my finger, and lost my cigarette lighter.

Now that I'm back out in the country where I belong, it isn't quite as convenient to run to the store for materials as when I was living out a fantasy on Bellevue. Round trip from where I hang my hat now is eight miles and in my car that's a good gallon of gas and a quart of oil.

Last Saturday I decided to start with something simple. You wouldn't think a repair job on a kitchen table leg would pose problems; and it doesn't unless you are Bo Whaley and have two deformed hands, five thumbs on each.

The table needed a leg repaired. I broke one off dragging it from upstairs to downstairs when I moved a couple of weeks ago. Ever watch a table do somersaults down a long flight of stairs? Very entertaining. A New Year's Eve drunk couldn't have done it as well.

It took me about thirty minutes to drive to town, buy nails, and have a cup of coffee with the boys. I really didn't want the coffee but stopped in for a visit hoping maybe somebody would ask me to play golf. Why? Because I was chomping at the bit to answer with, "Can't, I'm repairing my kitchen table."

Nobody mentioned golf so I just announced loud and clear to all present as I rose to leave, "If anybody comes looking for me to play golf, just tell 'em I'm home repairing my kitchen table!"

The telephone was ringing as I entered my house. I caught it on the third ring after knocking over an end table and busting a lamp shade.

"Hello!"

"Mr. Whaley, this is Mary at the restaurant. Did you leave a sack of nails on the table here a little while ago?"

"Uh, yeah, right. I'm gonna' repair my kitchen table, Mary. You see, I was moving and the table . . ."

Mary wasn't impressed and indicated as much with, "Right. Good luck. Whatcha' want me to do with these nails?"

I should have said, "Come on out here and repair this table with 'em." I didn't. I played it straight for a change. "I'll be right down to get 'em. Thanks, Mary."

An hour, another gallon of gas and quart of oil later, I took my nails and headed home. "See y'all later. I've got to get on home and repair my kitchen table."

"How many kitchen tables you got, man?" a smart guy asked. "You just left a little while ago to go repair one."

"Never you mind, Buster! Whatever I got that's busted, I can fix," I countered.

"Why don't you try your hand on that ol' Mercury of yours, then?" another dummy called out.

I didn't bother to reply because I only talk to mechanics about my car. I do pray about it a lot though. Anyway, it's nearly impossible to relate to unappreciative audiences. They're a drag. Pearls before swine, you know.

With hammer and nail in hand, along with a handsaw, foot rule, and marking pencil, I tackled that fractured table leg. Since it was in three pieces, I used masking tape to hold it together for the nailing. So far, so good.

I found out pronto, however, that I was missing a badly needed tool, a vise. Ever try to nail pieces of a table leg together with the thing jumping all over your back yard? Heck, I started behind the welcome center and ended up in Jerry Gay's driveway across 441.

Then there was the kid on the bicycle who stopped to watch. I saw him staring at me. "Whatcha' want, kid?"

"Nothin', just watchin' you kill that snake," he replied.

"Ain't killin' no snake. I'm repairing my kitchen table. You see, I was movin' and . . ."

"Oh, I thought you wuz killin' a snake," he said as he pedaled off, disappointed.

I picked up the pieces and returned to my yard. Up she went on the picnic table. Put your foot on one end and the other tips up, thereby spilling nails, a foot ruler, handsaw, marking pencil, and half a can of Coke. And tell me this—why won't the saw ever start where you mark? I tried placing one of my ten thumbs alongside the thing to guide it like my Daddy used to do, but only succeeded in splitting a thumbnail. Also, try and find a Band-Aid when you need one, especially after having just moved. I can tell you, though, that masking tape will work in an emergency.

Want another tidbit? Putting half a concrete block on one end and sitting on the other won't cut it, either. Finally I had a brainstorm. No, strike that. I had a mental lapse, sticking one end of the leg in the outdoor grill, closing the top, and placing a brick and a half on it for good measure. Then I anchored the other end, which was on the grass, with my foot. You know what happened when I was half through that booger, don't you? The saw became pinched and I wound up dancing a polka with a broken table leg. Paul Anderson couldn't have pulled that saw out.

I finally dumped the whole shebang on the porch and opened a can of tuna for lunch before riding back to town to make a purchase.

"How come you ain't playin' golf?" asked a caffeine regular as I walked in.

"Not today, George. Too busy. Have things to take care of around the house. Fixin' tables and things like that," I said, poker-faced.

"Wish I could do things like that. I just ain't very handy around the house when it comes to fixin' things," he sighed.

"Nothin' to it, fella. Just have to put your mind to it. You know, shoulder to the wheel, nose to the grindstone and all that," I bragged.

I finished my coffee and made my purchase, a card table. Now then, if I can just figure out how to open it up without raising a blood blister on one of my remaining thumbs, I'll have it made. I can tell you this, it's a little spooky sitting on the kitchen floor with a card table before you, trying to shuffle a red five to play on a black six at 7:00 A.M., while waiting for the toast to pop up. But I'm gonna' enjoy my new card table if I can just figure out how to open up the legs.

Little Things Cause the Most Trouble

What's wrong with the world? I'm not sure, but every morning I listen to a front-table group of pseudointellectuals debate the question.

They debate such issues as inflation, the economy, the plight of the American farmer, Social Security, the federal budget, and nuclear arms. But these aren't the issues that drive you frantic day in and day out, produce sleepless nights, and cause divorces. They either knock you for a loop or Ronald Reagan takes care of them.

Rather, it's the nagging little things that cause all the trouble—little things like nothing is made right anymore, and nothing fits. Furniture comes apart when a special guest sits down and zippers get stuck (down) less than a minute before a scheduled speech before the local garden club or the Business and Professional Women's Club of Willacoochee.

TV programming has gone to pot. The one program you've looked forward to watching for weeks is postponed to make way for a documentary on Icelandic fishing and its importance to world economics.

People aren't reliable these days, either. Like the girl who promised you faithfully that she'd be there at noon to help out with your daughter's reception but calls at 11:45 A.M. to tell you she can't come because she's taking part in a mass baptism or attending a meeting of the part-time maid's association to vote on whether to affiliate with the teamsters.

It's things like this that warp the world.

You buy one of those TV discs that brings in 784 channels only to have the neighbor's dog chew the wire and instead of watching the finals of the Miss World Contest in Miami on the Playboy channel, the screen flashes a rerun of sumo wrestling in Yokohama on ESPN.

Things like this are never discussed at the front-table summit conferences.

There are some things that can bug a fella to the point of climbing on top of Dublin's skyscraper at South Jefferson and Madison, and shouting to all of Middle Georgia, "I'm mad as hell! And I'm not gonna' take it any more!" Like these:

• Warranties. They always take care of anything except what happens. Like when you take your new garden hose home and hook it up. The thing spurts water in every direction *except* in the direction of the rose bushes, for which you bought it. This is not covered. What *is* covered is that the hose won't ever shrink or straighten out.

• Medical insurance. Whatever the doctor tells me has to be done, the policy specifically exempts. You have to catch the disease *they* want.

• Buttons. Somebody, somewhere, is going to get filthy rich doing nothing but matching buttons. Every try to match a button on your blazer? They don't make them. You take your new blazer home and as you button the second button, your finger goes right

through the hole with the button on the end—of your finger. Is it
so hard to sew on blazer buttons and reinforce them? Not for you,
but for manufacturers it is seemingly impossible. A strong wind
will blow them off, but just try and remove the tag on the sleeve
that identifies the size of your blazer and see what happens. It
takes a crowbar, the strength of Paul Anderson, and the patience
of Job to do it. If only the buttons were sewn on as well!

• Kitchen utensils. There's the nifty knife sharpener that makes
a saw out of your favorite carving knife, the stainless steel flat-
ware that turns gray, the self-cleaning oven. Hah! I have one and it
doesn't work. Mine is just as dingy and grimy as when I moved in
last July. Consider other kitchen items, like free-flowing salt that
nothing can prevent from coming out except the slightest humidity
in the air; the "improved" ketchup bottle that produces no
ketchup until you bang it on the table, run hot water on its neck,
and stick a gray stainless steel knife down its throat causing a flow
of oooozzzy tomato stuff to run down your arm.

• What about whipped cream pressure cans? No problem. Just
shake them like the instructions say and thick, luscious, imitation
whipped cream squirts all over the cabinets, the wall, the dog, a
sampling of children, and two or three chairs.

• And those pickle jars with the easy-to-get-off lids? Simple.
Just take three different kinds of can openers, vice-grip pliers, a
screwdriver, one of those rubberized grabblers and see if you can
beat the machine that welded the lid on.

• I could go on and on, about water-resistant watches that stop
in a heavy fog; waterproof raincoats that get soaked and wet you
to the skin; the jim-dandy "easy-to-assemble" utility table that
has been around my house for three years waiting for a graduate
engineer or a master cabinetmaker to put the thing together; and
anything that operates on batteries.

• Then, there is the company that sends your bill with the reminder that "if not paid by the 10th, we will tell your mother-in-
law," along with a self-addressed envelope for your remittance—
and the remittance won't fit in the envelope.

What's wrong with the world? I'm not real sure, but a relative
newcomer has joined the world of child-proof medicine bottles,
glass patio doors, and television commercials: the computer.

You know about computers. They're the little devils that con-
spire against writers annndd dheir ded-lebel bes tu messs up
anithing ad eberthengg yu tri tu rite.

The Trouble with Vending Machines

I have a continuing feud going with coin-operated vending machines that refuse to do what they're supposed to do. Half the time they don't work, and when they do they don't deliver what I paid for.

I pull the lever for a candy bar and get crackers. I pull the lever for chewing gum and get potato chips or pork skins. More often than not I drop four dimes and a nickel in the slot, pull the lever designated for a Snicker, and nothing happens. I jiggle the coin return thingamajig and get back two dimes and a nickel. Where the other two dimes go, I'll never know.

Try and find somebody who will take the responsibility for it and see what happens:

"We don't know nothing about it. We just lease the space to the vending company," is popular. "You'll have to speak to Mr. Warbucks, the manager, about it. But he's on a cruise and won't be back for three weeks," is another.

You stand the same chance of getting your money back from Warbucks as you would from a television evangelist.

Here's another urge to go on a break and destroy mission prompted by coin-operated vending machines: After pulling the lever, the item I want, always up top, falls off the Empire State Building and gets caught in a mass of twisted wire about the eighth floor or ends up crossways at the entrance to the exit chute and won't budge no matter how much shaking and kicking I do. And a hand won't go up into the chute far enough to grab it. Trust me. I know this to be a fact.

Coin-operated vending machines offer an endless variety of items, from stamps to nail clippers, soft drinks to peanuts, cigarettes to self-portraits, and . . . newspapers.

Ahhhhh . . . newspapers. Not only do the darn machines play tricks, but some of the folks who fill 'em are a day or two late now and then. This happens to me with alarming regularity, especially in Birmingham:

I always stay at the Radisson Inn on top of Red Mountain in Birmingham. It's nice, has a great gym and workout room (that I've never used in the five years I've frequented the inn). There's only one feature I don't like about the Radisson: the newspaper machines.

In the first place, I always arrive late at night and follow the same routine. I search for an hour or two for my room, unload my clothes, and go for a newspaper. But the machines are located in a dark corner on the ground floor, and the newspapers inside are barely visible.

Now, here's the kicker: I insert my quarter, remove a newspaper, and walk back to my room where I settle down in a chair with a reading light over my shoulder. Somewhere along about Page Seven, Section C, what I'm reading has a familiar ring to it, as well it should. There I sit reading the newspaper on a Tuesday night, the same one I read the night before in Montgomery!

There's nothing more aggravating to a newspaper addict than to buy Monday's newspaper on Tuesday.

Finally, a word about coin-operated coffee machines. They are programmed at the factory to tilt the cup forty-five degrees. You put your forty cents in, select the desired combination of cream and sugar—black, black with sugar, extra sugar, cream, extra cream and so on—and then stand back and watch. The little cup, about the size of a thimble, falls from outer space and sits sideways, at a forty-five-degree angle, while half your purchase goes in the cup and the other half disappears down a drain installed for just such an occasion.

Then try to slide the glass covering up to remove the half-thimble full of coffee at the same time. Two will get you one that the hot stuff will saturate your shoes or wrist watch should you succeed in removing it from the machine.

Automation ain't really all that great.

Part 4

Maude, My Marauding Mercury

Do automobiles have personalities? After experiencing the joy of owning a Medicare Mercury, I have concluded in the affirmative or you bet your alternator they do.

Clunker Gets Two Parts to the Mile

ANYTHING MECHANICAL IS absolutely terminal for me. Like trying to do minor repairs, for example. I get all set, only to discover that my machine is Japanese and my tools American, or vice versa. Ever try to remove a 9/16-inch bolt with a fourteen-millimeter wrench? It'll send even Mr. Goodwrench scurrying for tranquilizers.

This is about my latest catastrophe, my twenty-one-year-old car.

I bought it six weeks ago and was determined to do it right this time. Scheduled to go to Atlanta for two days, I took it in to have everything checked. Four hours and $123 later I drove out of the shop sporting a new water pump, two new belts, a new water hose, a DIPZ-8355 and a pair of 8A-19549-As, prepared to tool it on up to Atlanta.

Did I say Atlanta? Hah! I tooled it not quite two blocks when the sound of a Sherman tank roared from under the hood. So, back in for another look-see. Ten minutes later, I was on my way again.

"Just a minor adjustment," he said, flashing a Dale Carnegie smile. "Have a nice trip."

I did. I had a great trip. To Atlanta? Nope. To Allentown! Both my new belts came off, resulting in the loss of power steering, so I pulled into a truck stop. Fifteen minutes, a cup of Me-Ma's coffee and five dollars later, I was on my way again. To Atlanta? Nope. To Stockbridge! My belts were off again.

"Won't do no good to put 'em back on. They ain't gonna' stay. You got a warped pulley," the man at the Gulf station told me.

So there I sat, twenty-five miles from Atlanta, with a warped pulley. I just figured to heck with it and drove on into Atlanta sans power steering. Ever drive in Atlanta for two days without power steering? Good luck and happy motoring! For once I was glad I didn't have bulging biceps. My little ones ached bad enough.

I finally made it back to Dublin, had the warped pulley straightened, and the fan belts replaced. No charge. Next morning, at the mall, the radiator did a Mount St. Helen's imitation. Diagnosis? Stuck thermostat. Treatment? Thermostat transplant. Eleven dollars.

I drove my nightmare two full days before the transmission decided to get cute. Put the gear shift lever in Drive and the car would sit there, moving when *it* decided to move. Diagnosis? Bad modulator valve. Treatment? Modulator valve transplant. Cost: $33.57.

I drove away with a brand new FX-102, but the car moved when I decided to move for a change.

My next out of town trip was to Wrightsville. Beautiful! Absolutely no trouble going or coming. (I rode my motorcycle.)

I'd had the car a total of seven days and had shelled out $174.57, but read on.

Next came a dead battery at the Chamber of Commerce. The city manager jumped me off and I drove to the nearest service station.

"Dead cell. Got to have a new battery," was the diagnosis. I decided to get another opinion, from a specialist.

"The alternator's shot," the specialist said.

One alternator: $41.20.

Are you believing this?

Next day I went to the golf course and on the way home no less than three cars pulled up beside me to tell me my muffler and tailpipe had fallen off. While I appreciated their concern, it was like telling a rock band in Macon they were annoying the neighbors—in Montreal! What the heck! I'd been listening to it all the way from the golf course. Ever hear a tape recording of World War II? That's it.

So, back to the shop for a tailpipe and muffler. Boy! The mechanics love me.

"I'll have it ready for you by ten tomorrow morning," one said.

I was there promptly at ten next morning. "Is it ready?"

"Not quite. Having a little trouble locating a fuel pump," he said.

"Did you say a fuel pump?" I asked in disbelief.

"Right. Take a look. Yours is leaking like a sieve."

Down on all fours, I verified it. Regular, at 1.15^9 per, was flowing like Lake Sinclair with the flood gates open!

"You wanna buy it? I've had it!" I told him.

"Well, yeah, I'll buy it. How much?" he asked.

"What'll you give for it?" I countered.

"Going price. Penny a pound," he said as straight-faced as a Saint Bernard.

Mistakenly, I rejected his junky offer.

Muffler, tailpipe, and fuel pump: $111.50. Total in twenty-nine days of ownership? $327.27!

All right, here's the kicker. Last Sunday night I went to a local restaurant for dinner. Finished, I exchanged greetings with the Bud Barrons and Ed Harpes and went to my car to go home. No deal. Not a sign of life. Jumper cables? Sure, I tried 'em. Might as well have used shoe strings.

The mechanic came and took a look. Diagnosis? "Your starter's shot," he said.

I haven't okayed the starter transplant yet. I'm checking with Medicare. The cotton pickin' car may qualify. In the meantime, I'm either going to take a penny a pound or find a guy who suffers the same chronic disease as yours truly: temporary insanity! Green stamps, food stamps, Raleigh Coupons? I'll take 'em!

My only other hope is that Ford Motor Company recalls all 1965 Mercury Marauders. Even if they do, I doubt seriously if mine can make the trip to Detroit.

Marauding Mercury Strikes Again

I'd like to thank those of you who've expressed concern and sympathy for my medieval Mercury. There's nothing I'd like to report more than to say she's doing fine. Not so, Mr. Goodwrench.

Two weeks ago I had to buy her a new pair of shoes and wiper blades for her bifocals. I figured she was in good shape. My mistake.

A week ago Friday was Black Friday for Maude Mercury. She had a relapse on me completely without warning. It happened like this.

I pulled into Ernest Todd's Pump and Pantry on East Jackson for fifteen dollars' worth of glucose for Maude. She took it easily and I was inside settling up with Ernest when he made his announcement.

"Must have just had your car washed," he said.

"Nope. Probably ain't been washed since Vietnam," I vowed. "Why?"

"Just lookin' at that stuff runnin' out of your car up front. Thought maybe you just washed it," he said, calm as a poker player holding three aces, with the fourth up his sleeve.

I looked at Maude and cringed at the sight. Ever seen a down spout in a rainstorm? That was the sight.

Down on all fours, I reached under the car and ran a forefinger through the puddle. Then, I did a brilliant thing. I smelled the reddish liquid, as though the odor would tell me something.

"This ain't water, Ernest!" I shouted. "It's sort of a reddish color—and greasy!"

A customer joined Ernest in chorusing the reply. "Transmission fluid!" they harmonized.

I patted Maude on her trunk lid and pulled out. Sounded like a Poulan chain saw under the hood. I drove to the courthouse and made a right turn. Sounded like a McCulloch chain saw under the hood. I finally made it to North Jefferson where a hitchhiker spotted me and ran behind Jefferson Street Baptist Church.

"Pray for Maude!" I yelled to him. But he didn't slow down. Last time I saw him he was hurdling a fence on to North Franklin Street.

In a matter of minutes, I had ground my way to Maude's doctor, Dave Brinson at Brinson's Chevron Service Station, who has her complete medical history on file.

"Think I need a little transmission fluid, Dave," I announced. He performed a preinduction physical and decided to operate.

"Pull her in the bay and let's get her up on the ramp," he said. It was then that I knew Maude was in serious trouble. Once on the operating ramp, it's surgery for sure.

His intern, Danny, was assigned to the case. He examined her block and made his diagnosis.

"Freeze plugs are leaking. All four of 'em," he said.

"Be honest with me, Danny. How serious is it? Go ahead, I can take it," I assured him.

"Two of 'em I can't get to. Have to replace 'em. Motor has to come out," he said, deadpanned.

"I can't take it!" I cried.

"And, another thing, she's dehydrated. Power steering unit's completely dry," he added.

With no disrespect to the intern, I requested another opinion. He called in Dr. Dave who took a quick look under the light and said, "Freeze plugs are leaking. Motor has to . . ."

"All right! All right! I heard! I heard!" I bellowed.

I mean, he was talking about a $300 job on a $30 car. Even Jimmy the Greek wouldn't take those odds. Like wearing Izod socks with combat boots.

As I stood contemplating my dilemma, with six dollars and an overextended MasterCard in my pocket, a stranger waiting to buy mineral spirits came to my rescue.

"This yours?" he asked with a frown as he peeped under Maude's hood.

"Yeah, I'm afraid so," I replied, flipping through my six ones, fingering my MasterCard and contemplating forgery.

"What's the trouble?" he asked, sincerely.

"Transmission fluid's leaking out," I said, giving it to him straight.

"Yeah? I bought an old '55 Chevy last year for $150 and had the same trouble. Fella' told me to put a half a can of brake fluid in the transmission. I did and it held up for eight months," he said.

Eight months! Heck, I'd settle for eight days!

So in she went, half a can of brake fluid. Right into the old transmission. Must have worked because it quieted the Poulans and McCullochs.

Now I'm afraid every time it changes gears the transmission is gonna lock and skid all the way up to the radiator. Time will tell, I guess. Anyway, $3.28 for brake fluid beats the heck out of a $300.00 motor job.

Now my only problem is that every time I cross a railroad track or go over a bump, the trunk lid flies up. It doesn't really bother me but I'll guarantee you it would scare the living hell out of a loaded bootlegger.

Brighter days are ahead for Maude Mercury, though. If my calculations are right, she'll qualify for Medicare in 1987. Meanwhile, I'll just keep pouring the brake fluid in her and go down the road with trunk lid a'flyin'!

Checkups Are a Pain in the Chassis

You've all been so nice to express concern and sympathy for my automobile (?) that the least I can do is bring you up to date on her condition. Maude would very much like to write to you herself but having just undergone her annual checkup, she's just not up to the task.

I took Maude in for her annual inspection last Monday at the Peacock Clinic. Dr. Minton handled the preinspection routine such as interrogation, filling out forms, etc. It went like this:

"What's her name?"

"Mercury. Maude Mercury."

"Middle name?"

"Marauder."

"Date and place of birth?"

"October 12, 1964 in Detroit, Michigan."

"Hmmmm. That makes her twenty-one, right?"

"Will be, if she lives 'til October 12."

"Residence address?"

"Wherever she knocks off."

"Is she covered by Mercurcare?"

"Right. Need the number?"

"Yeah. Gotta' have the number."

"O.K. 57BF6212B2314."

"Roger, got it. Does she have brothers and sisters?"

"Yeah, both."

"How many and their names?"

"Eight million. Let's see, there's Monterey, Marquis, Bobcat, Cougar, Capri, Zephyr . . ."

"I see. Planned parenthood was a no-no in the Mercury household, huh?"

"No doubt about that."

"Has Maude been hospitalized since her last checkup?"

"Oh, yes. She's been in the Brinson Clinic, the Chappell Institute, the Daniel's Evaluation Center, and the Bay Station Emergency Room. Also, every cotton pickin' service station between Dublin and Locust Grove."

"Hmmmm. What's the nature of her illness?"

"Everything from hardening of the armatures to low oil pressure."

"The old gal's been through it, hasn't she?"

"I'm afraid so. On top of all that she's been in Expensive Care at my house for the past four months."

"What seems to be the trouble?"

"All I know is she's a pain in the chassis!"

"Well, we'll check her out real good. Should take about thirty minutes."

After two cups of coffee, I eased back into Dr. Minton's waiting room. Apprehension was rampant and the expression on his face was morbid, only more so than usual.

"Come into my office. I've called in Dr. Gore, our specialist on hopeless cars, and he'll give you the prognosis. He'll be here in a few minutes, as soon as he finishes crying," Minton said.

"Crying?" I queried.

"Right. He's very sentimental. Hopeless cars get to him."

Dr. Gore appeared forthwith and within minutes had me crying, too. Not about Maude. It was the cigar that did it.

"I'm Dr. Gore," he announced.

"How do you do? I can almost see you. Is your emission control system broken?" I asked.

He ignored my attempt at humor, offering me a piece of his rope and a match. I'd have taken it but I couldn't find him.

"I like to come right to the point, Whaley. Maude is in sad shape. In fact, she's terminal," he said.

"Terminal? How can that be? I put new ones on as well as new clamps in July," I erupted.

"Well, here's the summary of my findings. Take a few minutes and read it over. No! Over here! I'm over here by the file cabinet. That's the coat rack you're reaching for," he said.

"I'm sorry. Sorta' smoky in here, Doc."

Dr. Minton opened a window and I was soon able to read Dr. Gore's prognosis. Disheartening, plain disheartening.

"Examination reveals severely ruptured kingpins and bushings as well as badly worn tie rods. The posterior lateral lugs are worn and threadbare and have caused a dislocation of the fourth cervical brake disc. Additionally, she is experiencing great difficulty retaining fluids in the radiator, transmission, and crankcase cavities. A previous modulator valve transplant and two cylinder borings have failed to grant relief in these areas. Her right eye is extremely weak on high beam as is the left eye on low beam. She also coughs a lot and groans when in reverse."

With the smoke cleared, I could see what appeared to be a prescription in Dr. Gore's hand.

"Is that a prescription for Maude?" I asked.

"Well, sort of," said Gore. "At least, it's a solution."

I took the prescription and tried to read it. It didn't make sense. All it appeared to be was a map with written instructions:

"Take Maude and drive twenty-six miles north on U.S. 441 to Irwinton. Hang a left on Highway 57 (if you make it that far) and go twelve miles to the Gordon turnoff at the intersection of 57 and 18. Hang another left on 18 and proceed one mile to the hazardous waste dump site. Brake to a stop (if the brakes are working) and get out. Reach in the window, put Maude in Drive and tell her goodbye."

"Is it really that bad, Dr. Gore?" I asked through misty eyes.

"Like I said, I come right to the point. It's that bad," he told me.

"You mean I don't get a sticker?"

"Son, you got stuck when you bought her."

"But, how do I get back to Dublin?" I asked.

Dr. Minton interrupted at this point, putting his hand on my shoulder and guiding me toward his office.

"Well, you see, Whaley, I happen to have this nice, clean, one-owner '76 Impala and . . ."

Stealing Maude May Be a Hanging Offense

I know you're as tired of reading about my Medicare Mercury as I am of pushing and begging it. Maude spends a great deal of her time resting and recuperating. I spend a great deal of mine walking and fussing.

Sometimes it's embarrassing to drive a twenty-one-year-old car and it definitely ain't in the social register. Take last Saturday for instance.

I went to a real nice brunch at the Dublin Country Club, one of those affairs where you put on foo-foo juice and shine your shoes. You know what a brunch is, don't you? It's what you do when you sleep late on Saturday morning after partying on Friday night and get up too late for breakfast and too early for lunch. Wonder what you call it when you really tie one on and don't wake up until 3:00 P.M., too late for lunch and too early for supper? A lupper, I guess.

At the country club I parked Maude as far back in the parking lot as possible, next to a dumpster.

Once inside, I began mixing and mingling and soon heard the voice of Joe Wingard behind me. He was whispering to his wife.

"It's embarrassing, Joe. We must have the oldest car in the parking lot," she said.

"No, honey, we're safe. I saw Bo Whaley here a few minutes ago and . . . ."

"Oh, really? Well, thank goodness for that," she sighed.

I've been trying for quite a while to decide what to do with Maude, but it's hard to dispose of a loyal companion. They keep coming back to haunt you.

A couple of weeks ago I was reading the latest FBI *Uniform Crime Report* figures for 1980. "Motor Vehicle Theft" caught my eye. In the past three years, 26,872 cars have been reported stolen in Georgia. How 'bout that? I decided to give it a try.

I woke Maude up, gave her time to stop coughing, and took her out to 441 and I-16. I wrote a note and stuck it under the windshield wiper along with a dime, three dollars for gas, and six dollars for oil, enough to get an interested thief as far as Allentown. The note was crystal clear:

Her name is Maude. Please wake her gently. She will probably start if you follow these simple instructions: jiggle the ignition key

three times to the left, then twice to the right; jump up and down on
the seat four times, kick the floorboard twice with your left foot,
and shake the gear shift lever vigorously back and forth between
"R" and "D-2" while rocking the steering wheel left and right. If
she fails to start, look in the back seat and you will find a sledge
hammer. Take it, raise the hood, and strike the motor block a
mighty blow just above the third spark plug to unclog the gas line,
allowing gasoline to enter the carburetor. Once done, drop the
sledge hammer, run like hell, and get back inside.

Repeat initial instructions. If she doesn't respond, try turning
the ignition key while slamming the left front door. This usually
knocks the dirtdauber's nest off the fuse box causing the light to
come on, thereby indicating she has power.

In the likely event she still won't budge, you have two choices,
Mr. Car Thief: (1) Use the dime under the windshield wiper to call
272-0822. Ask for Dave or Danny. Tell 'em Bo told you to call.
They know Maude and me well. There's a pay phone in the Holiday
Inn across the street. (2) Open the trunk. Do this by kicking the
broken right rear tail light. Inside you will find a fifteen-foot length
of rope. Then, do as I've been tempted to do so often. Select the
nearest tree, secure one end of the rope around your neck and do
what comes naturally.

One other thing, Mr. Car Thief. Profanity is ineffective, so save
your breath. Maude is obviously deaf.

It didn't work. Next morning I went to check on Maude. Still
there, asleep or dead, right where I'd left her. Under the windshield was my note; my original nine dollars; eleven more, and a
hastily written note; saying, "I gave at the office"; plus three
sympathy cards. The dime? Gone. The way I figure it the guy
called Central State Hospital about 4:30 A.M. and is probably at
this writing studying ink blots and weaving baskets. The rope is
still in the trunk. Car thieves just ain't got no guts, I guess.

I took my $10.90 profit and put this ad in the paper:

Wanted: Good home for classic 1965 Mercury Marauder. Answers sometimes to name "Maude," but speak up. Many extras
such as floorboard; steering wheel; horn ring; front and back seats;
door handles (8), four inside and four outside, three work; gear
shift lever, slightly worn; four tires; a hubcap; rear bumper; three
unbroken windows and half an unbroken windshield. Hurry and be
first. Best offer gets this gem. Write care of *Courier Herald*.

The offers came fast and furious. Unbelievable! Here are the
three I'm currently considering:

"My offer is $50 to take Maude off your hands. No checks. Send cash or money order. Will come and get her upon receipt of money."

"You can bring her to my place providing you pay the tow charges. Just put her in the barn along with my 1938 Terraplane. They should get along fine."

"If you can wait until October, I'll take Maude off your hands. Our school, Hillcrest Elementary, has a Halloween Fair every year and our most popular exhibit is the one where, for a dollar, to vent your frustrations, you can beat an old car with a sledge hammer. (Leave the sledge hammer in the back seat or no deal.)

Any more offers? I feel conspicuous standing here on the courthouse lawn under a big tree holding a 15-foot length of rope. Please hurry!

Maude, the Medieval Mercury, Is Still Clunking Along

A car salesman stopped me on the street a few weeks back and popped the question right in front of the F&M Bank.

"Bo, when are you gonna' get rid of that car? I've got a real nice one out on the lot I'd like to show you," he said.

"Sorry. Can't buy no car," I admitted.

"Why not?"

"Well, I ain't rich enough or poor enough to buy one," I explained.

"What do you mean, not rich enough or poor enough?" he asked.

"Well, it's this way. If I was rich enough I'd just buy a car, write you a check for it, and drive it home. If I was poor enough the gov'mint would buy me one. As it is I'm one of those unfortunate devils in the so-called middle-income group who has to make out best he can."

Children probably come as close to calling things the way they see them as anyone, including baseball umpires. Take the case of Hank, the seven-year-old son of a Dublin druggist and his wife.

Hank is a handsome lad and bright beyond his years. The boy is very observant, too, as demonstrated by this little episode, which is absolutely true.

About a month ago, I was having dinner at the front table in my usual haunt, when Hank and his parents were preparing to leave after finishing their dinner. (Hank had also cleaned off a couple of tables. He is also very smart.)

His parents paused to exchange pleasantries with yours truly and others at the front table while Hank went outside on the sidewalk to explore West Jackson Street, as seven-year-old boys are prone to do.

Within seconds, Hank bounded back inside, yelling to his mother, "Mama! Guess what! Rag-mop is outside! Come and look!"

So what's a mama to do? She went outside with Hank to take a look and returned in a flash bordering on hysterics.

What was Rag-mop? None other than my medieval Mercury, Maude!

Correctly assuming that an explanation was in order, Hank's mama stopped laughing long enough to offer this one.

Rag-mop was a 1951 Ford, fifteen years older than Maude. It belonged to Hank's mama, Ginger Tomlinson, who drove it all over Ocilla when she was Ginger Land and winning beauty contests there as well as leading the high school band as a pretty majorette. She even took it with her to college when she attended South Georgia College in Douglas and the University of Georgia.

"That old car was as much a tradition at home as gnats and potatoes," she said. "All the majorettes more or less adopted it and gave it the name, 'Rag-mop,' the title of a popular song when I was in high school. My son, Hank, has seen it many times on visits back home with Luther and me, and he loves it. I guess when he saw your Mercury parked out front, he immediately identified it with my old Ford—Rag-mop."

Like I said, children just have a way of calling things the way they see them and when he saw Maude he was really seeing Rag-mop.

While kids are very observant, they are also easily impressed, especially when it comes to cars. This little episode is also true.

Early last summer, I took a little motorcycle trip to Savannah and, as usual, I rode out to Savannah Beach. I can no more go to Savannah and omit the beach than I can go to Atlanta and not have coffee in the Hyatt Regency's Kobenhavn Coffee Shop. (They do things with eggs there that would make the hen smile.)

While at the beach, I was approached by a youngster, about twelve, and his Dad, about thirty-five. Both were interested in my motorcycle, which is a beauty, if I do say so.

"Sure is a pretty motorcycle," said the boy.

"The boy loves motorcycles and cars," said his dad.

"Thank you, I really enjoy it," I replied. "I'll take you for a little ride if your dad doesn't mind."

He didn't, and we did. We rode about two miles.

Once back with his dad, the conversation shifted to cars and I knew the inevitable question was coming.

"What kind of car do you have?" asked the boy.

"Marauder," I said nonchalantly. "I drive a Marauder."

"Oh, yeah? Golly, Dad, did you hear that? He drives a Marauder!" said the youngster, duly impressed. "I bet it'll really fly, huh?"

"It just might, son. Any day now—and in all directions," I told him.

His dad just smiled but didn't blow my image, or Maude's. He knew, though. He knew that the Ford Motor Company hadn't made Marauders in years—many years.

EPA gas mileage ratings really don't concern me. I'm more interested in how far a 1965 Mercury Marauder will travel on a gallon of glucose.

Ol' Maude's Fire Is Beginning to Burn Low

Following Maude's last public appearance in March, when she rolled in the Saint Patrick's Parade, I took her back to the Intensive Car Unit at what was formerly the Dublin Welcome Center. She shares a semi-private bay there with her sister, Matilda, my thirteen-year-old Mercury Marquis.

Maude seems to be resting quite comfortably, although she still has considerable difficulty retaining body fluid, as well as three quarts of Quaker State 10-W-40 a week. But in spite of her medication, she still sputters and coughs a lot and runs a high fever when I take her out for her weekly run on Sunday afternoon.

Of course, I have to be realistic about Maude, realizing that she's nearly twenty-one years old and will no doubt be moving on to that big grease rack in the sky before long. Although it's inevitable, it's hard to accept.

Maude really had a close call about a month ago when some thief stole her heart (a Sears Diehard). I'm convinced she would have died had it not been for the quick action taken by Dr. Paul Watson of the famous P. M. Watson Heart Clinic and Radiator Repair on Jefferson Street.

Thanks to Dr. Watson, and one of his interns, her life was saved when a pacemaker (a used Firestone) was transplanted. A 1976 Buick Electra 225 was the donor and she's been in the Intensive Car Unit since the transplant.

It's really disheartening how some people have no respect for the down and out. I mean, just a friendly word now and then would undoubtedly do wonders for Maude's voltage regulator, not to mention what an occasional pat on the hood would do for her morale.

Two separate incidents last week really set Maude back a ways. I'll never understand how some people can be so cruel and heartless.

First of all, last Sunday, I pulled in and parked Maude in a parking space near the entrance to the Holiday Inn. My mother and I went inside and had lunch, like we do every Sunday. It was when we came out that Maude was insulted. Here's what happened.

As I was backing Maude out of her "handicapped only" parking space, some New Jersey American remarked to his wife, who was about the size of a house trailer (double wide), "The guy probably can't read. It says 'handicapped only' as plain as the nose on your face, right?"

"Right. Some people just don't care, Tony," replied the double-wide.

Now then, had those remarks come from some good ol' boy from some nice place like Fort Deposit, Alabama, Sumpter, South Carolina, Pascagoula, Mississippi, or Willacoochee, Georgia, I'd have thought nothing of it. But from a pair of Aces from Hoboken, New Jersey? No way was I going to pass up the opportunity.

"You talkin' to me, Slick?" I asked greasy Tony.

"Nah, just tellin' my wife how you parked in a 'handicapped only' parking space. You'd never get away with that in Hoboken," Tony said.

"Well, I challenge both of you to show me a more handicapped car than Maude and if you can, I'll apologize," I shouted as I backed out and started to drive off.

"What? Hey, that sign don't mean reserved for handicapped cars! It's for handicapped people!" Tony screamed.

"Yeah? And say hello to your mama 'n 'em up in Hoboken!" I called back to him.

Many people have giggled and snickered at poor Maude in the past two years. Some have gone so far as to call her names and make faces at her. But the ultimate insult came by mail last week.

I joined the Dublin Elks Lodge last month and received my first lodge bulletin last Thursday. I anxiously read the announcements until I read this one:

> We are certainly glad to have Mr. Bo Whaley join our lodge. Only thing, Bo, if you drive "the car" to the lodge—please park in back.

I'll tell you, friends and neighbors, that really cut to the quick. The thing that hurt most though is that with an attitude like that on the part of Exalted Ruler Wayne Lewis toward Maude, she'll never be inducted into the Elks Auxiliary.

Part 5

All in the Family

Families—we all have one. This section provides an insight into mine.

Daddy's Little Girl Starts Growing Up

I FACE A WALL COVERED with photographs, mostly of my daughter, Lisa. I see one taken when she set a school record by scoring 1000 points in her basketball career; one sitting on her throne when she was named Homecoming Queen in 1976; one of her receiving her diploma the night she graduated; and her official senior photograph. I'm prejudiced, but I think she is the finest and most beautiful daughter in the world. She inspires me every day of my life.

Lisa has given me so many happy moments that to try to list them would be futile. I reflect on some of them every day.

Like trips to Daytona . . . ghost stories late at night, with her hiding under the bed . . . weekends in Atlanta and dining at the Midnight Sun . . . her first car . . . train rides on the *Nancy Hanks* . . . sitting up all night talking and telling jokes.

And, just last week she was here for the play, *Look Homeward, Angel,* and saw her daddy-hero floundering around on stage—a hopeless drunk. (I am proud that that is the only time she has seen her daddy in such a condition.)

The pictures on the wall tell a story, the story of transition from little girl to young lady: the trampolines and toys turned to Toyotas and television; the Mouseketeers became The Young and the Restless; mama's old hats were replaced with cream rinse and hair rollers; and daddy's seat at the ball game, the movie, on the boat, and at the restaurant is now occupied by somebody else—Lisa's date.

Yes, no doubt about it, my little girl just up and became a young lady, a beautiful young lady. I'll never forget the night that the realization hit me right between the eyes. It was truly a date to remember. And I do. It happened this way.

I drove down to David Emanuel Academy in Stillmore to see her play basketball. She was a sophomore, age fourteen. I always followed the same routine when I went to see her play. I sat and watched the girls' game with a friend or two and Lisa would come and sit with me for the boys' game. As far as I was concerned, this night would be no different. Boy! Was I wrong!

David Emanuel was playing Bartow Academy and the girls won their game easily. I walked to the concession stand between games. (I actually didn't want any coffee, but I couldn't pass up the opportunity to gloat as Lisa had played an exceptionally good game.) After finishing my coffee, I strutted back to my seat to wait for her as I always had. And true to form, she came bouncing up the bleachers as radiant as a sunrise. I shifted in my seat to make room for her. That's when she hit me.

"I've got a date, Daddy. I'm gonna' sit with Robert!"

Well, sir, I didn't know what to say! I don't think I could have spoken anyway with my heart in my throat! My little girl? A date? The little girl who just last year, it seems, sat on my lap and pulled at my glasses; went to sleep with a Barbie doll in her arms and a Pekingese, Chen-Chen, lying beside her; ran as hard as she could and jumped in my arms when I got out of the car when I got home from work; giggled all night when Audrey Ann or Debbie spent the night with her and I scared the pajamas off both of 'em with ghost stories and ugly faces; drove my car when she was twelve (and drove it well); walked hundreds of miles in high heel shoes playing "grown-up?" And now, she has the nerve to grow up on me and have a date? Unbelievable!

I really don't recall very much about the ball game, but I can sure describe Robert to you in full detail.

I watched Lisa as she left me to take her seat beside him. I wanted him to be ugly, with pimples, long hair, ears like Dumbo, and a nose like Pinnocchio, but he was a nice, clean-cut young man. I should have given Lisa the credit she deserved. I should have known he would be a nice boy. But I watched him like a hawk, anyway.

I tried hard to hear what they were saying as they giggled back and forth but the cotton pickin' fans wouldn't be quiet so I could hear. Nevertheless I maintained my surveillance until the half when I eased back to the concession stand. I had to have a cup of black coffee and a few cigarettes! As I was devouring both, I saw them coming, Lisa and Robert. She was smiling from ear to ear, and I felt like cutting his throat from ear to ear! He had moved the old man out and had him singing the old song, "Somebody Else Is Taking My Place."

With a cigarette in one hand and a cup of coffee in the other, I met Robert. I tried to remain calm and collected as I shook his hand and came out with a bald-faced lie.

"It's nice to meet you, Robert."

He shook my hand firmly and looked me right in the eye as he spoke.

"It's nice to meet you, Mr. Whaley. Lisa has told me a lot about you."

Con man, I thought. *What a con man. He ain't gonna snow me!*

"Would you and Lisa like to go to the Dairy Queen after the game and get something to eat?"

"Oh, no thank you, sir. We're going to a dance."

I felt weak, again. I could see the picture forming in my imagination. He would put her in the front seat of that hot rod with the mag wheels, lifters, tape player, portable bar, four-in-the-floor and take off like Cale Yarborough as his oversized wide-ovals slung gravel over the gymnasium. I would be able to hear him "get" all four gears as he roared out of town with the tape player turned up as high as it would go!

I was wrong, again.

I walked with them to his car, a conservative Chevrolet Impala. I felt like apologizing as I watched him open the car door for her and walk around to the driver's side and shake my hand again. He made a big point with me when he said, "I'll be careful, Mr. Whaley, and I'll have her home by 11:30."

I poked my head in the window after he was seated under the steering wheel and gave him a firm pat on the shoulder.

"Just call me Bo, Robert. All Lisa's friends do."

I watched him drive away, with my life in the front seat, and as his taillights disappeared from view, so did things like trampolines, ghost stories, train rides, mama's old hats, The Mouseketeers, Barbie dolls, trick or treating—gone. I had greeted my little girl when I arrived for the game and watched her ride away, a young lady.

Truly, a date to remember.

I look again at the wall above my typewriter and see some empty spaces, spaces for more pictures: one of her graduation from Georgia Southern; one of her as a "little sister" for the Kappa Sig fraternity; one as its sweetheart; one of her on her wedding day, and, yes, there is a lot of space left on the wall. Who knows?

Being a House Guest Has Its (Dis)advantages

This will be a short dissertation on the advantages (or disadvantages) of being a house guest. I write from a recent experience.

I was in town for the State AA Basketball Tournament at Georgia Southern College. My daughter, Lisa, who lives in Statesboro said something to me that made sense.

"Why don't you spend the night at my apartment tomorrow night? I'll cook dinner for you after the games."

What's this? Lisa, my little girl who always thought braised beef ribs was a bovine respiratory virus and veal scallopini a New York Mafia chieftain, was going to cook dinner for me? No way was I going to pass that up.

I need to point out that Lisa doesn't live alone. She and two other beauties, Sonja Simmons and Cindy Zable, share an apartment.

Lord, I don't know what will happen when one of them decides to marry. I can just hear the wedding ceremony now: "Do you take this man to be your lawful wedded husband?"

"I do . . . but only on the condition that Whaley and Zable are included in the deal."

The three girls are very religious—they worship each other.

Have you ever been apartment hunting at eleven o'clock on a Saturday night in the rain? You haven't? Hop in.

First, get directions from your daughter, then completely disregard them. If you don't, you'll end up sitting in front of a bank in the parking lot of Statesboro Mall in your Mercury while she sits in her Toyota in the parking lot at Statesboro High School. And unless one of you makes a move the situation could prevail on into eternity.

I made the move, calling her apartment from a nearby Big Star. Zable answered and gave me directions, a horrible mistake. But then, on the other hand, I've never been to Cleveland on a rainy Saturday night.

So, I went apartment hunting, searching for Apartment 3, 103 Valley Road. Sounds easy, right? Wrong! Friend, I could get lost in the Lincoln Tunnel.

Oh, I found the apartment complex right off, right on Valley Road where it was supposed to be. The problem was that all the buildings are identical.

Lisa finally caught up with me, rescued me, took me off the merry-go-round and to her apartment where Randy Brown, her friend and mine, was busy barbecueing chicken. She chipped in with baked potatoes, onions, garlic bread, and iced tea. The three of us enjoyed a delicious meal at 12:30 A.M.

I appreciated the hospitality afforded me by Lisa and her friends. They spared no effort to make me feel right at home. They even saw to it that newspapers and magazines were strewn all over the floor, put dirty dishes in the sink, dropped dirty clothes wall to wall, and hid all the clean towels. They also let me sleep on the sofa (You see, Lisa has been a house guest at my pad, too).

I need to mention here that a fourth occupant resides in Apartment 3, 103 Valley Road—another pretty female. Her name is Honey, and she is a six-month-old golden retriever who retrieves things like my socks, shirt, shoes, Lisa's slippers, Sonja's pajama top, Cindy's jeans, my newspapers, and odd-lot blouses and pantyhose. It has reached the point now where Honey would also have to be included in any wedding deal.

One of the problems in being a house guest is not being able to find anything, like a water glass at 2:00 A.M. when you wake up and your tongue feels like the Chinese army marched across it earlier in the evening wearing muddy combat boots.

At my house finding a glass is no problem. I just pick up a half a dozen dirty shirts, three pairs of pants, half a dozen newspapers, and an armload of dirty towels and there's my glass. It's been there since Labor Day.

At Lisa's you open the cabinet where the glasses would normally be and find cassette tapes, a notebook, a pair of ballpoints, one sock, and a flea collar, but no glass.

And who moved the bathroom? At 4:00 A.M. you stumble over a chair, trip on a bottle, and step on a hair roller enroute to what should be the bathroom door. Open it and there's one of the cutest little clothes closets you'll ever see.

Why didn't I turn on the light? Because I couldn't find the switch, that's why!

Waking up on a Sunday morning can be quite an experience for a house guest, too. I felt a warm and tender, though somewhat sloppy, kiss on my mouth, nose, cheeks, and chin. The thought that one of those lovelies planted it there trickled across my mind but the shocker came when I slowly opened my eyes only to look eye to eye, head-on, at a golden retriever named Honey who still hadn't figured out exactly what I was doing there in her bed.

Enter Lisa, head wrapped Arablike in a turkish towel.

"Good morning! Wanna' take a shower?" she asks.

"Yeah, great," I reply as I crawl off the sofa and Honey crawls on.

"O.K., head of the stairs, first door on your right. Here's a clean towel."

After negotiating the stairsteps and finding "the first door on my right," I proceeded with my Sunday morning shower. But it ain't as simple as it sounds.

In the first place, the towel holder ain't really a towel holder at all. It's a hair dryer and pantyhose holder, and I learned right quick that those aluminum pegs that hold hair rollers on the sink underneath will burn you. Hot ain't the word. You could light a cigarette on 'em.

I moved on to the tub but faced another obstacle.

A shower curtain rod holds a shower curtain, right? Wrong! In Apartment 3, 103 Valley Road, Statesboro, Georgia 30458, a shower curtain rod holds more pantyhose, towels, bathcloths, shower caps, and a host of unmentionables that have twisted straps that hang down and drip.

Crawling in and out of the shower at Lisa's apartment is like walking through a beaded Chinese room divider. It's all part of being a house guest.

I thought about my visit all the way back to Dublin on Sunday afternoon. What could be better than being twenty-two, beautiful, and having your own apartment along with two good friends? Only one thing.

Being her Daddy!

A Father Will Eat Crow for Daughter

Several years ago, I manned my typewriter and wrote these words:

"I can assure you that I have no intention of ever setting foot on this campus again!"

They were written after I'd returned from Georgia Southern College where I witnessed the crowning of the Homecoming Queen, Patrick Fetter, a male.

To whom was the statement made? Dr. Dale Lick, president of Georgia Southern. It was not uttered in jest.

The next year another queen was crowned at the college. I have no idea who it was as I wasn't there and saw no publicity regarding the homecoming activities other than a mention on the sports page that Georgia Southern lost the basketball game, again, to Murray State.

Three weeks earlier, I had received a late night telephone call from my daughter, Lisa, a junior at Georgia Southern. The call went like this:

"Hey, daddy! Whatcha' doin'?" she began. "Did I wake ya' up?"

"Oh, no. I had to get up to answer the telephone anyway," I assured her as I glanced at my watch, which showed 1:25 A.M.

"Good! I didn't want to wake you. Just wanted to tell you the news," she spurted out. "Wanna' guess?"

(News! You fathers of daughters know what happened then don't you? Right! My imagination jumped on a roller coaster and I fired the questions at her, playing the guessing game at 1:27 A.M., while trying to light a much-needed cigarette with an injured Bic.)

"You're married?"

"Nope."

"Divorced?"

"Nope. You're not even close."

"You made an *A* in psychology?"

"Come on now, don't be ridiculous. Give up?"

"Yeah, I give up. Lay it on me, Lisa."

"I don't know if you're ready for this but I've been nominated as one of twelve girls in the Homecoming Queen contest this year!"

(Pause. . . . Long pause.)

"Daddy? Hello, Daddy? You still there?"

"Yeah . . . yeah. I'm still here, honey. It's just hard to talk with a half-smoked Winston in my throat. Did you say you've been nominated for the Homecoming Queen contest at Georgia Southern or am I having a nightmare?" I gasped.

"Right. The voting is next Thursday. They'll pick six for the finals and . . ."

"Well, I hate to tell you this but you know with a name like Whaley you don't stand a chance of a . . ."

"No problem. The faculty can't vote."

"Good! How many boys in it?"

"None. They're trying something new this year. All girls."

"Well, good luck, and keep me posted," I said and hung up.

Back to sleep? No way, Rip. I had a problem and I knew it. If she won, where could I find a good recipe for crow?

I was fast becoming desperate as the days passed. No way I wouldn't be in the Georgia Southern gymnasium the night of January 26th if Lisa was standing there as one of the Georgia Southern Six.

Just as I was on the verge of panic, another call came. Lisa again. It was the day after the voting.

"Hi! Well, you can rest easy. I didn't make the final six," she told me.

"Why not? Was the faculty allowed to vote this year?" I asked.

"Nope. Just didn't make it. It was fun though. When're you comin' to see me?"

"Uh, soon. Yeah, I'll be down to see you soon. We'll go out to dinner. Anywhere you like."

"Great! I'm about ready for a good steak," she said.

"You can count on it. Steak! Anything you want—except crow! I don't want any crow so . . ."

"What'd you say? Did you say *crow?*" she asked.

"Forget it. Just thinking out loud, honey. See you later."

"Right . . . I'll, uh, see you later, Daddy. But, you did say *crow,* right?" she asked in a very confused tone of voice.

And, who was the Homecoming Queen? I don't know. They didn't seem to publicize it much after the previous year's disaster.

Long-awaited Phone Call Finally Arrives

Late night or early morning telephone calls are not unusual at my house, especially when my daughter, Lisa, is on the other end of the line.

"Daddy! Whatcha' doing'?" is a typical 2:00 A.M. greeting from Lisa. "Didn' wake ya' up, did I?"

"Me? Wake me up? Nah, I had to get up to answer the telephone anyway."

I'll tell you, Lisa will dial at the drop of a credit card, but it's always great to hear from her. I remember some of her calls well. Like these.

1976: "Daddy! Guess what? I've been elected Homecoming Queen! How 'bout that? Homecoming is Friday night. Can you come?"

Can I come? Does Grizzard like grits? Is the pope Catholic? Can Evel Knievel ride a motorcycle? I wouldn't have missed it if I'd had to walk the 200 miles to David Emanuel Academy and back. I went, stood, cried, and watched my little girl crowned Homecoming Queen.

1976: "Daddy! Guess what? The coach says I only need two more points to go over 1000 for the school record. We play Tuesday night. Can you come?"

Can I come? Is New York big? Will a rattlesnake bite you? Can Herschel Walker run? Of course I went and watched her score numbers 999 and 1000, and the game was stopped while the coach presented her with the basketball.

Now, we move from David Emanuel Academy to Georgia Southern College.

1978: "Daddy! Guess what? I'm a little sister!"

"Yeah, I know. And you have been for nineteen years. Your brother, Joe, can vouch for that."

"No, no! I'm a Kappa Sig little sister. They voted tonight. How 'bout that?"

How 'bout that? Kappa Sig made a good choice.

1980: "Daddy! Guess what? I'm a sweetheart."

"Yeah, I know, honey. I've known that for years."

"I mean Sweetheart of Kappa Sig. I just learned."

"You just learned at 2:15 A.M.? Congratulations!"

Kappa Sig made another good choice.

1980: "Daddy! Guess what? I got lavalliered last night."

"What! Who did it? Just tell me who did it! I'll break his neck! I'll kill him! You just take it easy and try to get some rest. I'm on my way. Oh, have you reported it to the police?"

1981: "Daddy! Guess what? I got pinned last night."

"You got pinned? What the heck? Lisa, I didn't know you were on the wrestling team. You shouldn't keep things like that from your daddy. Now then, here's what you do. If she's got you on the mat with a crossbody lock you can break that with . . ."

"Come on, now. I was pinned by Randy."

"Randy? What're you doin' on the boys' wrestling team, Lisa?"

And I remember one more call. I remember it very well. I guess maybe I'd been expecting it for the last twenty-three years. It came a week later on a Saturday morning.

"Daddy! Guess what?"

"I give up. What?"

"Randy gave me a diamond last night. We're engaged."

Pause . . . Pause . . . Pause.

"Daddy! Daddy! Are you still there? Answer me . . . Daddy!"

"Uh, yeah . . . yeah, I'm here, baby. Uh, congratulations. I'm happy for you, real happy. Randy's a fine boy. I couldn't have made a better choice for you. When are y'all comin' to see me?"

"Next week. We'll be there next week, O.K.?"

"Fine. See you then."

I hung up, went to my bedroom, and cried. Tears, real but happy tears. My little girl had made the biggest decision of her life, and Randy had plucked the fairest rose in the garden.

Lisa and Randy came over the next Monday night. We broke

bread together and celebrated their engagement—Randy, a handsome young man, and Lisa, a beautiful young lady, with their lives stretched out and waiting. Randy will enter medical school, having graduated from Emory. Lisa will support him, encourage him, and boost him along the long and rugged road to his M.D. degree. He'll make it and go on to become a fine doctor.

I couldn't help but notice that Lisa, wearing her engagement ring, had changed. The girl has all of a sudden become left-handed after nearly twenty-three years as a right-hander. Things that she's always done with her right hand she suddenly must use her left for: scratching her nose, rubbing her forehead, straightening her necklace, yawning (she must have yawned 300 times and it was only 8:30), adjusting her earring.

Then, there's Randy Brown. He is a Kappa Alpha, but he has a lot in common with the Kappa Sigs. He makes good choices.

Lisa? She makes good choices, too.

Lisa and Randy go well together. I'm sorta' proud of both of them. Besides, they're both good friends of mine and I like that.

Groom-to-be Learning about Discrimination

I usually avoid weddings like the plague, having attended one too many in my life. But in recent weeks I've become a little closer to the rice, bouquet, garter, and miniature sandwich affairs. That can easily happen when your child is involved.

I learned one thing for sure—for dang sure—that males have a well-founded discrimination gripe when it comes to the wedding merry-go-round. Here's why.

Wedding plans for Lisa Whaley and Randy Brown were announced October 20 and that started the bridal ball rolling—for the bride. The groom? Left in the jetstream, honey. And the newspapers told us all about it with these headlines from the date of the announcement until the December wedding.

"Whaley-Brown Wedding Set for December 19."
"Kitchen Shower Given by Friends for Miss Whaley."
"Linen Shower Honors Bride-elect, Miss Whaley."
"Country Club Cocktail Buffet for Miss Whaley."

"Lingerie Shower for Miss Whaley in Statesboro."
"Afternoon Tea Fetes Miss Whaley, Bride-elect."
"Breakfast for Miss Whaley Given by Friends of Bride-elect."

All right, so much for the bride-elect and her prenuptial she-nanigans. But what about the poor groom-elect? Have you ever seen these headlines with reference to the groom?

"Frog-gigging Honors Groom-elect, Mr. Brown."
"Fish Fry Fetes Groom-elect, Mr. Brown."
"Friends Throw Beer Bust for Groom-elect, Mr. Brown, Who Is Presently Out on $1,000 Bond."
"Jr.'s Supper Club Is Site of Oyster Roast and Shrimp Boil for Groom-elect, Mr. Brown."
"Craps and Poker Party at Doc's Cabin on Ohoopee River Honors Groom-elect, Mr. Brown, Who Lost Honeymoon Money."
"Vienna Sausage, Potted Meat, Pickled Pig's Feet, Saltine Cracker, RC, and Moon Pie Buffet at Johnson's Store in Stillmore Honors Mr. Brown, Who Is Reportedly Recuperating Nicely in Room 220 at Emanuel County Hospital."
"Chitlin' Supper Given by Friends of Groom-elect, Randy Brown, in Cobbtown Tobacco Barn."
"Fruit-of-the-Loom Blowout in Twin City Honors Groom-elect, Randy Brown."

The ink hadn't dried good on the newspaper announcement of the wedding plans before the little card so familiar to all who frequent jewelry stores appeared in Swainsboro and Dublin stores. It read like this:

Bridal Preferences of Lisa Whaley:
China—Apple Blossom (Haviland)
Crystal—Old Galway by Galway
Casual China—Lancaster (Wedgewood)—Stonehenge White
Stainless—Beaded Antique (Towle)
Casual Crystal—Lenox (Virginia Blue)—Fostoria
Sterling—Old Master (Towle)

There you have it. All for the bride. But how about the groom's preferences? Is he to be overlooked completely? Heaven forbid! I took care of that by putting out a few lists on behalf of the groom in appropriate bait, tackle, and beer stores, as well as other likely locations, in Dublin and Swainsboro. Here they are:

Groom Preferences of Randy Brown:

Beer—Pabst Blue Ribbon or Stroh Light
Underwear—Fruit-of-the-Loom or Jockey; Shorts, Size 36—T-shirts, size 44-46 (V-neck, please)
Reels—Zebco 33, Zebco One or Ambassador 5500-C
Rod—Lew's Speed Stick
Lures—Rapala, Rooster Tail
Live Bait—Crickets, Shiners, Louisiana Pinks
Tobacco Products—Skoal (snuff); Vantage (cigarettes)
Shirts—Gant or Enro, Size 16-33
Trousers—Sansabelt, Size 36 and beltless
Socks—Burlington, midcalf
Coat—Size 46 regular
Notice: Gift certificates accepted

I was immediately pleased to learn that the groom received two six-packs of Stroh Light from Estes, three pairs of Fruit-of-the-Looms from the Imperial Men's Shop, one Zebco 33 and a gift certificate for 200 crickets and a quart of Louisiana Pinks from Oconee Bait and Tackle, two cans of Skoal from Clyde at the Red Circle, and two Gant shirts from the Sir Shop. And more was forthcoming.

I mean, what's right is right and after all the cotton pickin' groom-elect has been discriminated against and passed over in the wedding merry-go-round far too many years. It just plain ain't right.

Wedding Parties Can Take Their Toll

It is almost June. My mail reminded me of it last Friday—double envelopes, you know. Double envelopes? Right, wedding and graduation invitations. They always come in double envelopes, with a little piece of toilet tissue covering the invitation, to add a little class, I guess.

Graduation invitations really pose no problem. Graduation is a one-shot deal. March in—be seated—stand up—walk—grab the diploma—shake hands—switch the tassel—and a senior is transformed into an alumnus. While he may not be able to spell *alumnus,* the moment he accepts that diploma he becomes one.

Weddings are a bit more complicated and drawn out. They run on and on for months until the wedding ceremony (double) rings down the curtain on the marital scenario.

From the date of the engagement announcement to the wedding day, there's a whole lot of shakin' goin' on. Like engagement parties, teas, showers, breakfasts, cocktail buffets, champagne brunches, rehearsal parties, groom's dinner, and wedding reception—and most are laced with booze.

I made the trip through the marital twilight zone with my daughter last fall, to a December 19 wedding. From October to December, parties of one kind or another were held all over Middle Georgia, and this posed a problem for one uncle of the bride, Don Henchley, a farmer, hunter, and fisherman from Cobbtown.

Don and his beautiful wife, Jo Ann, didn't miss a party. They came early and stayed late. And when December rolled around, Don was still rolling with the flow.

It was at a December party given by the grandmother of the groom that I heard Don spill his tale of woe and elaborate on the problems of his whirlwind social life to a group of men in the den.

"I'll just tell you, Hoss. I don't know if I can hold out 'til th' weddin'," he said.

"Why not? What do you mean by that?" the groom-to-be asked.

"Well, it's like this. At my house, it's got to where when I get up in th' mornin' an' see Jo Ann ironin' my white shirt, I just ask her one question," Don said.

"What's that?"

"Jo Ann, where are we gettin' drunk at t'night? She tells me and tha's it," he explained, shifting his glass from right hand to left. "I got four weddins' an' a class reunion—all in December— not t' mention Christmas and New Year's Eve. More'n likely my two bird dogs figger I been kidnapped, and my shotgun's got cobwebs in th' barrel. Heck, I been t' some sort o' weddin' shindig ever' night since September and I'll be dadgummed if I ain't 'bout run out o' gas."

I hadn't seen Don Henchley since my daughter's wedding reception until last week when I saw and talked to him briefly in a Metter drug store where he was having a prescription refilled.

"How's it goin', Don?" I asked.

"Rough, Bo. Rough as a cob. I been tryin' ever since New Year's Eve t' get my stomach straightened out," he grunted.

"What seems to be your problem?" I asked.

"I figger it was all them little sausage balls and cheese concoctions that done it. Man, I didn' have a square meal from September 'til New Year's. I ain't eatin' no more o' them things," he groaned.

"You mean the kind served at Lisa and Randy's wedding reception?"

"Uh huh, an' at 'bout twenty-five or thirty parties 'fore that," Don said.

"You don't reckon all that liquor and champagne, along with the sausage balls and cheese, had anything to do with it?" I asked.

"No way! Ain't no liquor ever been made that'll tear a man's stomach up like mine's been," he swore.

"Medicine doing you any good?"

"Don't know, but I'm scared to stop takin' it," he whimpered. "But, I c'n tell ya' one thing for sure, good buddy."

"What's that?"

"Any more, when I wake up in th' mornin' an' see Jo Ann ironin' my white shirt, know what I do?"

"No idea . . . what?"

"I tho' my two bird dogs in th' back o' my pickup and head f'r th' woods—and don't come back home 'til after dark. I figger it's safe in th' woods 'cause ain't nothin' t' bother ya' there 'cept rattlesnakes, an' I can handle them. But them weddin' parties and class reunions? Nothin' but a mess o' sausage balls an' cheese things. An' they'll kill ya', Hoss. They'll flat out kill ya'," Don said as he limped out of the drug store toward his pickup with Jack and Jill, his two bird dogs.

And I couldn't help but wonder. . . . Was Jo Ann possibly ironing Don's white shirt when he woke up that morning?

The Sweetest Christmas Carol Ever

I never thought I would hear a Christmas carol more beautiful than "Silent Night." I hadn't—until last Christmas Day.

It was midmorning and I was having coffee with those dearest to me. My mother was there and looked beautiful in her red dress and coat. She was having fun, again. So was I. And then, a surprise!

Through the kitchen window I saw the car pull into the driveway. Out jumped my daughter, son, daughter-in-law and grandson! They had arisen early to drive to Dublin to be with me Christmas morning. Oh, I know, this scene repeats hundreds of thousands of times every Christmas morning, each one singularly special. Mine was no exception, except that it was my scene.

Live and learn. Ever said that? It's true. How about all those electronic toys and games you shopped for hours on end and when you found them, paid $29.95 each? And the $24.00-worth of batteries you bought to make 'em work? Did they make the little fella' jump up and down? Maybe, maybe not.

I know the feeling. I was through shopping and stopped in at a neighborhood drug store to visit friends. While there I spotted an obscure, but eye-catching, little plastic toy on the shelf. It was simple. A plastic hammer and two plastic pegs. It's function was obvious. The price? A whopping $1.69! I bought it as an "extra." You know, just so the kid would have another package to open. At age two and a half he couldn't have too many.

You're way ahead of me, Grandpa. Of all the boxes he tore into you know the one he played with most, don't you? And the one he held in his arms when he had to leave later to go see his other Grandpa? The hammer and pegs? Right!

There was one other he got a big kick out of, a toy helicopter. You know, one of those that you pull a string and a round thing zooms skyward? It really wasn't the helicopter zooming skyward that turned him on. Oh, no! It was watching Granddaddy Bo go up the tree after it zoomed skyward but then not earthward. Grandchildren sure make us old folks do strange things, don't they?

While everyone else was having refreshments in the den, I had mine. I scooped little Jeremy up and eased to the back of the house. Just the two of us. Grandpas like it that way. (So do grandchildren, thank goodness.)

We searched around and found a water bed. At least it was a water bed to me. To Jeremy it was the Atlantic Ocean. Know why? 'Cause Granddaddy Bo said it was, that's why!

I threw the little fella' "in the ocean" and really had the waves rolling! Between waves and laughing so hard he had tears, little Jeremy sang to me the sweetest Christmas carol I ever heard:

"Do it again, Granddaddy Bo!"

(I plan to, little fella', and, if we can't find a water bed in Baxley, well, we'll just head south—to Florida and the Atlantic Ocean!)

Of course, it will take Granddaddy Bo a few days to recuperate from climbing trees, rolling and tumbling on the shag carpet in the den, and making thousands of waves in the bedroom. But, that's OK. My daddy did the same thing twenty-five years ago with little Jeremy's daddy, Joe. And I can almost hear him now. He must have said it a thousand times: "You know, we love our children; but we worship our grandchildren."

Thanks, Jeremy, for a beautiful two hours Christmas morning. I know many, many other granddaddys must have had a similar experience. And, I love your song: "Do it again, Granddaddy Bo!"

What Do You Do with Grandchildren?

Several years ago I heard a friend in Swainsboro answer the question.

"You love 'em and you tolerate 'em," was the way he put it.

He had just completed a three-week baby-sitting assignment with his three grandchildren, ages three, five, and eight, while his daughter and her husband vacationed in Hawaii.

Back at his usual haunt on Monday morning after the youngsters had left on Sunday, he relaxed over a cup of coffee at Key's Cafe.

"Good to see you back, John. Grandchildren gone?" he was asked.

"Yeah, they left yesterday," he replied.

"Bet you miss 'em, don't you?"

John didn't answer right away. He stirred his coffee, shifted in his chair, and then replied, smiling.

"Well, yeah. Yeah, I do miss 'em. But, oh what a sweet lonesome!"

*   *   *

I'm into the grandpa bit, having one that turned three not long ago. Did I go to see him? Yes, and, as always, the visit was too short.

I watched his daddy build a ship from little plastic pieces while the boy lay prone on the floor, watching, chin in hand. (Why is the camera never around when you need it?)

The ship had the tallest smoke stack I ever saw. It looked like an egg carton with the Empire State Building stuck in it, all 102 stories.

Next, my turn.

"You make one, Granddaddy Bo," he said, handing me a double handful of red, white, and blue plastic pieces with holes in 'em.

Build a better mousetrap? Nope. Build a higher smoke stack. I did. The Empire State Building now has 103 stories and is 1,250 feet, one inch, high.

What do you do with grandchildren? You play with them. Sometimes they'll nearly kill you, but you play with them. You forget your age and go ahead. You'll remember it next morning.

On my way home I thought about 'em, grandparents and grandchildren, and how we let the little rascals do things to us that start fights otherwise.

For example, you lift him up and seat him on your lap. He giggles and slobbers and you grin and wipe. It's called one-on-one. The world has stopped for a few moments. No one else exists.

Suddenly, and with the quickness of a snake's fang, he rips off your bifocals and slings them across the room! They bounce off the TV and land in the magazine rack.

Do you become violently angry, scold him, and banish him to his room? I think not, Gramps. More than likely you will say something like, "Hey Mama! Did you see that? He threw those glasses all the way across the room, and, left-handed! The kid's gonna be OK. Must be thirty feet or more across this room. Looks like you gotcha' a pitcher or a first baseman, son."

Next, it's Grandma's turn.

She spent two hours and twenty-five dollars at the beauty shop the day before the grandchildren, ages two and four months, arrived. Every hair is in place and colored (rinsed). Let it drizzle and she'll cover up like a turtle.

Her new dress compliments her hair-do as she sits with Grandpa in their favorite restaurant the night before the grandchildren are to arrive.

Wanna' see a mad Grandma? Just let the waitress brush past her and upset one curl or spill just one drop of milk on the shoulder of her new Jonathan Logan. Does she burn? She makes the microwave in the kitchen look like a refrigerator!

But next day, she'll feed that baby, let him pull every curl out, then lay his head on her shoulder. Jonathan Logan be damned. Then, she'll walk and pat—and wait—and wait.

Finally, here it comes! "Buuuurrrrppp!" Similac covers the right shoulder of a drowning Jonathan Logan. Is Grandma mad? Never!

"Didya' hear that? How about that? I'll bet he's never burped like that before, huh?" she brags.

Enter the daughter. "Oh, Mama! I'm sorry. All over your new dress and . . ."

"Bah! Who cares? Didya' hear him, Dianne? Hear him burp? Bet he never burped like that for you, huh. Wow! I'll tell ya' he's just . . . ."

"Buuuurrrppp!"

"See there! Isn't he something!"

Grandpa can't stand it.

"Here, let me have him while you get cleaned up. I'll just sit here and watch the ball game with him."

Grandpa dozes; so does baby. The ball game continues. Time passes. So do other things.

Suddenly, Grandpa is awakened by the realization that his new Izods are soaked! The same Izods he cautioned the store not to make the inseam too short on or he wouldn't pay for them. The same Izods that nearly cost the family cat his life for jumping on 'em with sharp toenails.

His mind is jarred in the brief moment of realization.

"My God! Somebody pulled the plug in Lake Sinclair!" he says to himself as he inspects and verifies it.

Son-in-law expresses dutiful concern.

"Darn, Henry! I'm sorry about that. Here let me . . . .

"No problem, Jeff. No problem at all. Nature, you know. And, hey! Look at that!" he says standing up with Lake Sinclair on his lap. "Man! The kid's got some kidneys. No kidney problem with this fella', Jeff!"

So, what do you do with grandchildren? Perhaps Otto von Bismarck answered it best and simplest when he said: "You can do anything with children if you only play with them."

I just hope my grandson Jeremy remembers that I made the highest smoke stack—and, he tore it down.

The Move—Because We Love Them

I can't really pinpoint just when I decided to write this, although the theme has tiptoed across my mind many times. It could have been when I had a recent conversation with a friend. We both shared a common concern: What to do about mama? Why? Because we love them.

Upon returning home later that evening, I was ready to reduce my thoughts to writing in the hope that my words, admittedly inadequate, might serve to help someone else, concerned about another mama, make a decision—because we love them.

I made mine within the past month. It was inevitable that I would have to make it. So far, I am comfortable with it because in my heart I know it was the right—and only decision—to make. That is important.

I had to remove a loved one from the confines of her home, the only one she ever owned, to place her in a care facility so that she might receive the attention she deserves.

It is done; she is there. We are comfortable with it. The long nights and days of indecision over. So why am I writing this? Simple. Because I know that there are literally thousands upon thousands of others who are faced daily with this same decision. The only question is just how long we shun the responsibility of making it. I am convinced that it may well be *the* major domestic concern in America. Why? Because we love them.

My decision was not a hasty one, and neither will yours be when you make it. There are certain definite and tell-tale signs that, individually, are insignificant; but, like snowflakes, when combined, they accentuate the passage of time and the necessity to pause and consider the options. Oh, we would like to turn the page and read another story to keep things in a form of status quo—like they used to be. We dream of a miracle and pray for guidance, and will accept either, because we love them. We eventually emerge from the confines of this "twilight zone;" we exit the world of fantasies and dreams and enter the world of realism, which is always there. Popular singer Jim Reeves echoes the feeling when he sings, "Make the World Go Away." It won't. We have to cope with it, and will, because we love them.

The signs? You'll see them. They sort of ease into your life—softly. Like when you first notice that it requires more and more effort for her to negotiate those two steps leading from the carport to the den; having to curtail the daily late-afternoon walks with her little canine companion, Mitzi, that both eagerly anticipated; not being quite strong enough to maintain her house and yard in the same manner she has been accustomed to for years, and with so much pride; finding it more and more difficult to sign checks, write a letter, or prepare her church envelope for Sunday morning, while you observe but remain silent. Partially because you don't know what to say, but primarily because you aren't prepared to receive her response—you are really treading water—you avoid the confrontation with the inevitable.

Days and weeks flit by. On visits you become acutely aware that a decision, a most important decision, is in the offing. Your observations become more microscopic and less discreet. Too soon they become fixtures in the reservoirs of your mind, only to surface later at seemingly the most unpredictable times and places.

In the middle of a hymn on Sunday morning you suddenly recall that she stumbled and nearly fell twice when you visited her the day before—once going into the kitchen and once coming out. As you ride to work you remember the words she mumbled when she tried to thread that needle to sew a button on your shirt the week before: "They just don't make the holes in these needles as big as they used to, son!" You smile and remain silent, still treading water. You just thread the needle for her and make yet another deposit in your memory bank.

As you watch a football game on TV you see those two bruised spots on her leg, that you should have asked her about.

Days become weeks, weeks become months. Your visits and your concerns become more frequent. And then, one day, you sit

down with her in the den and take a closer and longer look—
because you love her.

The needle holes continue to shrink; the impatient poodle
hasn't been for a walk in weeks and doesn't understand; there are
more bruised spots; the unanswered letters are beginning to pile
up on the coffee table, alongside a stack of unread newspapers; the
TV is as blank and mute as a shoe box; the refrigerator that once
overflowed with the likes of chicken, pork chops, steak, sausage,
eggs, meat loaf, vegetables of all kinds, and delicious homemade
pies, now houses only a slice or two of boiled ham, a carton of
milk, a partial package of wieners, and a frozen chicken pie. Tell-
tale signs? Definitely.

The time is fast approaching when a decision must be made.
You casually mention the bare refrigerator and she answers with a
weak smile: "Well, I just don't seem to get as hungry as I used
to."

However, she couldn't shrug off the bruised spots, the unanswered mail, the unread newspapers, the dormant TV, the ever-
shrinking needle holes, the neglected poodle, or the delinquent
church envelopes. Welcome back to the world of reality. The buck
has stopped, and you have it! The game of pass the thimble is over
and it has been dropped in your hands. You will handle it. You
will do what you must, because you love her.

What do you do? You tread a little more water. She agrees that
she needs help and you make a decision. You search and you
search and search some more until you finally locate a lady to
come, to help, to offer companionship. You are relieved, temporarily. You are comfortable in the knowledge that she is not alone
during the daytime and you make an honest effort at commuting
the fifty miles to be there at night. What you have really done is
buy a little more time while you wait for a miracle.

The arrangement works, but only for a little while. Her companion confides in you that she needs professional care. You knew
it but were waiting for another opinion. You weren't ready for it.
You never would be, because you love her. It is decision time
again.

As you sit with her in the den you try again to tread water, to put
off. You put water on for a cup of coffee that neither of you really
wants. You have the feeling that she is reading your mind.

You settle down with the coffee on your lap—Stone Mountain in your throat and the Sahara Desert on your tongue. It is a one-on-one situation, for you and Mama are the only two left. You have already made your decision. You would rather go to prison than relate it to her. But she's your mama, she can, and does, read you like a book. True to form, she makes things easier for you: "Son, I know I need some help. I'll leave it up to you. I'll do whatever you think is best."

The decision is made. From that point on it was just a matter of implementing it. Some call it "making arrangements." We did, and she is now in Dublin. I can, and do, see her every day.

So why have I written? To provide just a little insight into an area of concern that so many of us live with and, most importantly, to emphasize the need for "them" to fully realize that only one factor breeds our concern. We are concerned because we love them.

In My Father's Footsteps

Sunday, August 27, 1978, was a very special day for me. I went to the United Methodist Church in Scott, Georgia, to be the guest speaker at the homecoming service. The fact that I drove from Chattanooga the night before to be there is incidental. I would have driven from Sacramento, California, just as eagerly.

For me, that's where it all started some fifty years ago, the day I was born in the Methodist parsonage at Scott, where my father was beginning what would be forty-three years as a minister in the South Georgia Conference.

I walked to the pulpit with some apprehension and stood in the very spot where my father had stood so proudly as a young minister.

For forty-three years I walked in his footsteps, as a child in Scott and later, as I grew older, in his beloved Middle and South Georgia woods and fields hunting quail. If he stepped on a log, I stepped on it, right where he did because I knew he would not steer me wrong. He always seemed to know just where the shallow places were, and the deep ones. If I had adopted a theme song in those beautiful years, it would have been, "Where He Leads Me I Will Follow."

As we both grew older, his steps shortened a bit and slowed

down; but they were still *his* steps and I followed them until his death in 1969. He was my father. He was my buddy. He was my best friend. Do I miss him? Only twice every twenty-four hours—night and day.

The homecoming service was beautiful. As I stood in the pulpit and surveyed the scene, I couldn't help but reflect on days gone by. I was back in the atmosphere in which I had grown up, a small country church attended by good, hard-working and devout people. I wanted just to stand there and look at them. The character that radiated from their faces was so reassuring that I must have uttered a silent prayer that they stay that way. What I was really looking at was America, the way I think it should be. A few gathered together on Sunday morning to do the very thing this country was founded for them to do, worship.

No doubt there were many thousands of churches throughout America this morning that were more beautiful, with much larger congregations, but I feel certain that none was fostering the purpose for which it was built more than Scott Methodist, worshiping God. And I was there, standing proudly in the place where my father had stood half a century before.

The service ended with the singing of his favorite hymn, "Blest Be the Tie That Binds." I was still humming it as we all retired to the front lawn under the trees to partake of an American tradition, dinner on the ground. No restaurant in the world has yet come up with a menu to compare with a meal prepared by the ladies of the church. The flies were there but didn't stand a chance as the wooden-handle cardboard fans were there, too, compliments of Townsend Funeral Home.

I had to pause for a minute as I enjoyed a piece of delicious lemon cheesecake, my father's all-time favorite. I wished he could be there. I even told a joke or two, as he would have, but somehow they just don't come out as funny as when he told them.

What I am really trying to do is say a simple "thank you" to the good people of Scott for inviting me back to stand where my father stood, to walk where my father walked. I appreciate their allowing me to stand "in my father's footsteps." I just hope that someday I might have earned the right to do so.

A Special Thanksgiving Prayer

This Thanksgiving Day I will be at mama's. Where there used to be some twelve or fifteen of us there will now be only two, mama and me—and a lot of memories.

I recall turkey and dressing with all the trimmings; lots of noise and laughter; reunion with loved ones; and my daddy and me slipping away to see if we could find some birds or a rabbit. Whatever, he always made sure that I got the best shot. After I missed, he would kill it and call out, "Bo, you sure popped him a good one!" (I guess in such situations it was all right for the preacher to lie a little. And I'm sure that he knew that I knew that he knew; but, birds and rabbits can't talk, and neither did I. I'd just prance up to the house as proud as Davy Crockett and yell out, "Look what I killed!")

Confidentially, I'm positive that the grandmas, grandpas, mamas, aunts and uncles, cousins, and even the dogs that accompanied us knew, too. But their lips were sealed tighter than those of a Mafia godfather before a Federal grand jury. After all, grandparents, mamas, aunts and uncles, and even cousins have their code of silence, too. And my daddy? Those secrets of our days hunting together in the woods and fields went with him to his grave—the day before Thanksgiving, 1969.

What I wouldn't give if he and I could roam the countryside just one more time, tomorrow afternoon, and bring home the quail that "we" killed for mama to cook as only she can!

I'd love to prop my gun beside a fence and plop down beside him to partake of the delicacies of the quail hunter's table (usually a stump) consisting of Vienna sausage, potted meat, soda crackers, a piece of "rat cheese," an RC Cola, and a couple of cinnamon rolls.

I'd thump the cockleburs and beggar lice from the bottom of my wet hunting pants while he lit his pipe or the remains of the cigar that had lain dormant in the pocket of his hunting coat, with his dog whistle, since the last hunt. I'd listen again as I have done so many times while he related stories of how he used to "really get 'em" in Scott, Dudley, Danville, Oglethorpe, and many other places where we lived and hunted.

He'd get a faraway look in his eyes as he told me about the "best bird dog I ever saw," Don, the setter he owned in Scott when I was born. I must have heard him say it at least 300 times, "Son, you only have one dog in a lifetime like Don."

With the victuals consumed and the dogs rested, we'd reach for our guns, his Browning 16 and my Remington 12, and head out again to walk logs, wade through briars, and climb fences (he never helped me over one). There's a good lesson contained therein. Note that I didn't say he didn't love me. I merely said he didn't help me over fences. The way I see it, he was wise enough to realize that I would have to climb a lot of fences later in life when he wouldn't be there to give me a boost. Boy, was he ever right! But, I'll tell you something, he boosts me every day, and I miss him.

Mama and I will talk and have fun and give thanks to God tomorrow, Thanksgiving Day. I humbly invite each of you to join me for this Thanksgiving prayer:

Our Heavenly Father:

We come now to this Thanksgiving interlude with thankful hearts, fully aware of our shortcomings, which are many, and of our virtues, which are few. Teach us to channel our thanks for what we have into the calm and serene river of gratitude, instead of into the rampant and roaring rapids of grief for the things that we have not.

Open our minds and prepare our souls to be tolerant of those who do not believe as we do and grant us the patience and knowledge to guide and direct those who believe not at all. And Father, instruct us in the utilization of leisure so that we might use it wisely to survey the untold beauties of the universe and beyond.

We also pray this day that we, through your infinite wisdom, may come to the realization that love for our fellow man is truly a joyful experience and that love for our Heavenly Father is humanly indescribable but an absolute necessity if we anticipate eternal life, the final reward in the galaxy of gifts bestowed upon us through your boundless love for us.

Help us, O God, to attain such a lofty plateau in our relationship with you that we are totally aware of the fact that to accept the teachings of your only son, Jesus, as our goal for living, is only the beginning of our Christian life, not the culmination of it. May we continually strive through our daily experiences to achieve the peace of mind that comes through the realization that we can live comfortably with ourselves within the confines of our own conscience, the true judge and jury of our existence on earth.

Finally, we offer our thanks this day for the many blessings that you have bestowed upon each of us: the certainty that the sun will set and rise again; that the rain will come and the rivers will flow; that we are all equal in your eyes because you are a fair and just God; that the only way that any of us will not gain the eternal heritage of your heaven is to turn away from your outstretched and beckoning hand.

For your love and blessings, we are eternally thankful this Thanksgiving Day, 1978. May peace and love reign triumphant over strife and hate throughout the world and the coming year bring with it an even greater display of faith in Christianity than the world has ever known.

So ends our prayer this day. It is offered humbly but reverently, in the name of your only son, Jesus Christ. Amen.

Thanksgiving Day: A Day with Mom

It happens every time I pick my mother up at the nursing home to take her out. I hear the same song as we walk the hall, slowly, to leave.

"Have a good time, Mrs. Whaley!" they sing out as we pass each room. And some, without fail, add the verse, "It sure is thoughtful of you to take your mother out, Bo."

For more than a year now I've accepted their plaudits and taken my bows, returning regularly for encores—undeserved encores, I might add.

It happened again yesterday, Thanksgiving Day. I bowed and smiled, cautiously trying to keep my halo from falling off, as I escorted Mother to the familiar strains of the laudatory tune, "Have a good time, Mrs. Whaley!"

Ten minutes later we were seated in the dining room with mountains of turkey and dressing on the table before us. I looked around and found myself surrounded by the Hansley Horne table, the Wilbur Jones table, the Sarah Orr Williams table, and the Tal Orr table. I mused at the setting and stole a line from my friend, Ron Riley, "Where could I find better company?"

The waitress greeted us with, "It's so nice to see you and your mother out today. You sure are good to her."

I accepted her praise for what a good boy I was, bowing in

familiar fashion while checking my halo. I retrieved my napkin from the carpet and sat back down to reflect on the pretty lady seated across the table and the praise and plaudits that had come my way.

I stirred my coffee and gazed at the familiar face reflected in the cup, pausing to sneak another peek at my Thanksgiving dinner companion. She was busy and paid no attention to my stares (Actually she was wrestling with a turkey leg).

Then it happened. My halo fell to the carpet, replacing my napkin. I stopped stirring and began reflecting on my lady wrestler.

Wait a minute! Me? Good to my mother? An hour here or an hour there? A short visit periodically or an occasional trip to the mall? Hah! Let's focus the camera and get the true picture.

Isn't she the same lady who saw to it that there was always lots of icing left in the pan for me to scrape when she made my favorite chocolate cake? Then she scrubbed it off my face after I'd cleaned the pan.

Isn't she the same lady who went through the valley of death to bring me into this world over fifty years ago in Scott, Georgia? The same lady who cared for me, nursed and loved me, sacrificed so I might know the good life?

Isn't she the same lady who tolerated such critters over the years as white rats, goats, pet mules, turtles, pet chickens, snakes, rabbits, gophers, and dogs, attending their funerals with me when they died?

Isn't she the same lady who repeatedly put her longed-for dresses back on the rack and pulled jackets and shirts from another one, never bothering to let me know we were poor materially?

The picture was beginning to come into focus.

Me? Good to my mother? Hah! The halo lay dead on the dining room carpet.

She's the same lady who made mustard plasters and hot Vicks compresses, poured Groves chill tonic down my throat by the gallon every spring, bandaged and kissed stumped toes and mashed fingers, removed splinters, lanced boils, soaked sore eyes, and spread salve from my head to my feet. She bought salve by the ton. She had a medical theory: When all else fails, put salve on it. Calomel and castor oil, quinine and Dickey's eye water, I know about those things. I was spared the asafetida, though.

She put up with more teasing from me than a bouffant hairdo; played left field when my team was one player short; always did her magic trick every October, coming up with a few coins from out of nowhere when the county fair came to town. (She even beamed like an Academy Award winner when I brought home a ten-cent ash tray that I had spent a dollar to win by throwing rings over pegs.) Who signed all those report cards I was afraid to show to Daddy?

She played marbles with me and won most of the time, when all the other marble shooters had gone home; washed and mended my dirty, ragged britches with the hole in the right knee and pretended not to see when I sneaked my little bulldog Skippy under the covers when she came to say goodnight.

More? Sure, there's more.

Who always ate the dark meat and end pieces of bread? Who saw to it that when mail call came in such remote places in the South Pacific as Leyte, Mindanao, New Guinea, Guam, and Okinawa in World War II that my name wasn't omitted? Who sent such goodies as boiled peanuts, chocolate cake, and homemade fudge?

When I returned to the United States, who went to baseball games to watch me pitch when what she really felt like doing was turning out the light, going to bed, and nursing a sick headache? Who consoled me when I lost, and shared my thrill of winning?

I was looking at her across the table.

Me? Good to my mother? Bear with me.

Who took me in seven years ago when my wheels ran off and I was alone for the first time in twenty-five years? Mamas just know when you need them.

So, I ask you, who's been good to whom? I only know that the longer I focus upon her, the clearer the picture becomes.

What else can I say?

I picked up my halo off the floor, put it in my pocket, drove her back to the nursing home, and headed for my typewriter.

Thanksgiving? It was a great day . . . .

Take a minute, pause, and say, "Thanks, Mama." She'll understand. If you like, I'll lend you my halo. I don't really have any use for it anymore, now that the picture is in proper focus.

Thanksgiving Day Brings Back Bittersweet Memories

When this rolls off the press I should be in or near the small town of Sparta in Hancock County. I've been there on November 25 for the past seventeen years. It's a special day to me. It's the day I buried the greatest friend I ever had. On November 25, 1969, my mother and I sat and watched as my daddy was buried in the Sparta Cemetery.

I'll do the same thing today that I've done every November 25 since 1969. I'll go and sit and reminisce. Once again I'll follow him through the woods hunting quail, stand by his side and listen to his fox hounds bark their way through the branches of Macon County, wait as he patiently untangles my fishing line or dislodges the hook from a tree limb hanging over the Flint River.

I'll sit at his grave and once again listen to the great stories he told while sitting in front of Dan Kleckley's store in Oglethorpe in the late 1930s. I'll hear him tell again how he won the Georgia State Liar's Contest with a story about his favorite rabbit dog and how surprised he was to see the headline in the *Macon Telegraph:* Methodist Preacher Wins Liar's Contest.

I'll have to smile when I recall the time he stopped preaching in the middle of a sermon in Alma and said, "Bo, go spit that chewing gum out."

I'll recall, too, the only time I ever ran from him when he was going to whip me. I ran under the house, only to get all tangled up in his trotline. He spent the better part of an hour removing fish hooks from my hands and seat. This done, he whipped me.

Then, there was the Saturday afternoon when he caught by boyhood friend, Jack Smith, and me smoking in the balcony of the Alma Methodist Church. I'd rather have tangled with his trotline. He whipped me, and Jack's daddy whipped him. I'll be thinking about that, too.

How can my visit be a sad one when I think about things like the Christmas many years ago when we were all at Grandma's house. It was Christmas Eve and all fifteen visitors had gone to bed. The presents were stacked neatly under the tree, appropriately marked. There were name tags like To Mama from Ruth, To Papa from Wales, To Margaret From Grace.

He got up and eased downstairs, pen in hand, and changed all the name tags so that they read, From Walker.

Christmas morning his little scheme worked well—for a little while. With his sister, Ruth, playing Santa Claus and giving out the presents, every one she picked up read From Walker. Grandma, Grandpa, Margaret, and Grace were all thanking him for their presents. He simply smiled and accepted their thanks.

In his early morning haste, however, he had written too fast for fear of being caught and his bubble burst when Ruth finally picked up a package which read To Walker—from Walker, proving that even the greatest of practical jokes slip up now and then.

I'll laugh, too, as I sit at his grave and roll over in my mind the note I found in one of his Bibles. It was written by him on the day I was born, with copies sent to his mother, father, and six brothers and sisters. It is a typical example of the humor and wit of my friend and father.

Scott, Ga.
December 11, 1927

Well Hello:

We are the proud possessors of a fine eight-and-one-half pound BOY this morning at eight thirty. Leila is doing fine and the BOY has a splendid set of lungs. What makes me feel so good is that Leila is o.k. and the BOY is perfect in form.

God has wonderfully blessed us and we hope to make a bishop of this BOY. I am so happy I could almost shout this a.m.

Don (my bird dog) does not like the BOY much, but I feel sure he will get the good feeling from his master in a few hours when I take him hunting.

Dr. Fort says that Leila is doing the best he ever saw a young mother do. Also, he says the BOY is perfect.

Well, I will tell you the truth. He is ugly; looks like uncle Henry Collins, the ugliest man in Hancock County. Ha, Ha. But don't you dare tell me that when you see him because it wouldn't do for a preacher to get engaged in a fight.

Will try and write a letter next week if I'm back down to earth by then. Pray for us that we may do what God would have us do and be the mother and father that He wants us to be.

Love to all. Yours devotedly.

Walker

A sad visit? No way. I'm just thankful that I had the benefit of his friendship and guidance for forty-two years of my life.

Next November I'll make the trip to Sparta again and relive the good times. When I do that it is hard to remember the bad ones.

Part 6

Observations and Conclusions of a Small-town Columnist

It has been said that daily newspapers tell you what's happening, and the weeklies tell you who's doing it.

The same is true of columnists. The big city boys tell you things like who's boozing it up behind Geeslin's Cotton Warehouse; we small town typewriter peckers go a step further and tell you where he threw the bottle.

Suuuuuuurrrrrrrrppppppp!!

The Darndest Game of Poker I Ever Witnessed

THEY CALLED IT "Las Vegas Night" at the "club" in this town where I was visiting a friend, who invited me to have dinner there as his guest.

We were still picking our teeth when a group of ladies gathered and took their seats around two tables pushed together with a large salad bowl in the center. They broke out a deck of cards and Dorothy commenced to deal to Ellen, Willa Mae, Jeannie, Merline, Francine, and Beatrice.

"Dealer's choice—first Queen deals," she announced as she flipped the cards around the table.

"First Queen? You mean first Jack, don't you?" interrupted Raymond, Ellen's husband, an observer and financier.

Dorothy never broke stride, continuing to deal without bothering to grant Raymond even the courtesy of a reply. But the look she fired at him would curdle milk and scare rattlesnakes.

The coveted Queen fell in front of Ellen the second time around, prompting her to say, "Probably the only thing I'll win all night."

As Ellen shuffled, Jeannie mumbled, "I sure hope we don't play all those crazy wild games like we did last week. What are we playing, Ellen?"

"Heinz 57," Ellen replied matter-of-factly, while casting a cautious glance at Raymond.

"Good," Jeannie agreed. "I just hate all that wild mess."

Raymond tried to remain mute as his wife dealt a hand of Heinz 57, but his curiosity got the best of him.

"Heinz 57? What the heck is that, Ellen?" he asked.

"Oh, it's just a game we made up. Seven-card stud with tens, twos, and fours wild. Tens are wild in the hole for Geminis and Sagittarians, twos are wild on top for anybody born between July 4th and Labor Day, and fours are wild up or down for anybody not born in Georgia. Jacks are wild in the hole for singles, Queens up are wild for wives, and Kings are wild up or down for divorcees. The Ace of Spades in the hole wins half the pot and one-third if turned up. One-eyed Jacks are double wild cards. Any questions?" Ellen asked.

There were none.

Raymond? He was last seen shuffling off, shaking his head and mumbling, "Lord, I love her; I married her; but I sure as heck don't understand her—Heinz 57?" (He would join Willard and John, husbands of Willa Mae and Beatrice, respectively, at the pool table.)

"Good luck, Ellen!" Raymond called back over his shoulder.

"Thanks, Honey. I just hope I break even tonight," Ellen replied.

"Break even? What do you mean, break even?" a more puzzled Raymond asked.

"Because I need the money," she said.

And Raymond shook his head.

Francine won the Heinz 57 hand with ease, seven nines, and the deal passed on to Willa Mae, who chose to deal "straight seven-card, one winner, nothing wild but the dealer."

"How do you play that?" asked a puzzled Beatrice.

"Easy, nothing to it," replied a confident Ellen as she reached in the pocket of her shocking pink jeans and pulled out a small, green memo pad bearing these notes on the cover:

Two just alike—Pair; Two just alike and two more just alike—Two pair; Three just alike—Three of a kind (Trips); Five all in a row—Straight; Five in same suit all mixed up—Flush; Three just alike plus two more just alike—Full house (Boat); Four just alike—Four of a kind; Five in same suit all in a row—Straight flush; Ace-King-Queen-Jack-Ten all in same suit—Royal flush.

"Oh," said Beatrice. Meanwhile, the ever-observant Willa Mae checked the contents of the salad bowl and barked, "Who's not in the bowl?"

"I left in," vowed Francine.

"I know I'm in 'cause my dime hit Jeannie's glass, bounced off Dorothy's ash tray, and went in the salad bowl," explained Merline.

"I put two nickels in and they're the only ones in the salad bowl," swore Ellen,

"Well, you've still got two nickels in your pile, Ellen," Willa Mae challenged.

"So what? I had four nickels to start with. Raymond gave 'em to me and . . . ."

"Yeah, big spender that Raymond. Sometimes a dollar won't last that boy a week. He just goes right through it," ribbed Dorothy.

"Well, I don't think Jeannie's in," announced Beatrice.

"I dern sure am in! I put in first," Jeannie yelled.

"Then you gotta' match the pot, Jeannie. You put in out of turn," explained Dorothy.

Reluctantly, Jeannie paid her fine, was put on probation, and Willa Mae dealt "seven-card, one winner, nothing wild but the dealer."

Ellen won. She took it all, after checking her research book, with "five in a row." (Beatrice came in second best with "three just alike," but without a reference book.)

After two hours, Raymond, Willard, and John strolled in and Beatrice immediately put the bite on John for five dollars.

"Five dollars? Heck, Beatrice, I've already got six mortgages on my truck and you want poker money? It's time to go home, anyway. I've got to get up at five o'clock to go fishing," John ranted.

"Well, give me a dollar, then, for one last hand of 'showdown' before we leave."

Good ol' Beatrice took the salad bowl money with "three just alike and two more just alike."

"That's a boat, Beatrice," said Ellen, peeping at the cover of her little note pad.

"Golly, Ellen, I wish I understood this poker as well as you do," a beaming Beatrice said as she dumped the contents of the salad bowl in her purse.

Beatrice left, but the game continued. Like John said as they left, "one monkey don't stop no show."

And that's poker, folks, the way the ladies play it, little green note pad and all. They do it a little differently don't they, Mr. Hoyle?

And remember, Raymond, first Queen deals.

You Can Get an Education on the Telephone

Recent news reports about the government secretly monitoring telephone calls set me to thinking about the telephones we had when I was a small boy. Almost everyone who grew up in a small town or on the farm had a "party" line, which meant that several families used the same telephone line.

It also meant that everybody on that line could keep up with the news of everyone else. We called it eavesdropping.

I guess I've done quite a bit of eavesdropping in my lifetime. I'm sure my activities had their beginning with the telephone party line in and around Oglethorpe. You see, after we got our telephone (a six-party line), I went to school from 8:30 A.M. to 3:30 P.M. and received my education from 4:00 P.M. to bedtime, on the telephone. And I'll tell you, it's hard to hold your breath for hours on end.

I learned some startling and revealing things by eavesdropping on the party line. For instance, I was among the first in the Oglethorpe area to know that Margaret Holder and Elvis Shurling were secretly married; that "Miss Cat" Allen had been brutally beaten and killed in her home right down the street from where I lived; that the Williamson brothers, Grady and Louie, were planning to take Doyce Mullis and myself "snipe hunting." (I refused to go, but Doyce spent a lonesome Saturday night in a ditch in the woods between Oglethorpe and Andersonville.)

I also learned that C. D. Etheridge and his first cousin, C. L. Barfield, had a "secret" hideaway up above C. L.'s daddy's garage; that Christine Holloway, the prettiest girl in the county, was going to the Methodist Youth Fellowship party with Edward Coogle. (I could have shot Edward for taking the girl I was planning to marry in fifteen or twenty years on the hayride.) Lord! Christine Holloway would have made Brooke Shields look like Phyllis Diller, with acne.

What else? Well, I found out Mrs. Pennington's "secret" recipe for strawberry preserves when she threw caution to the wind and gave it to her daughter, Patricia, in Americus over the party line. And I heard about Polly Randolph's problem with Raymond Duggan before her mama did. Also, that Carolyn Batten was wearing Elvis Andrews' class ring and meeting him "secretly" at the swimming pool in Montezuma on Saturday afternoons.

Eat your heart out, Hedda Hopper!

I learned all that via the telephone party line at the Oglethorpe Methodist Church parsonage. And if I'd been manning the telephone in my upstairs command post as I should have been during the early morning hours of December 7, 1941, I'd have known about Pearl Harbor and been able to warn our troops in Hawaii in advance of the Japanese sneak attack. You see, Mrs. Torrence would have told Mrs. Webb because there just wasn't nothing that Mrs. Torrence didn't know, and she told Mrs. Webb everything.

Remember the Albany tornado in the late 30s? I was among the first to know. Mrs. Torrence told Mrs. Webb and me.

I'll tell you, it was a sad day for us professional eavesdroppers when the party line bit the dust. Our Oglethorpe telephone should be in the CIA Hall of Fame, along with Mrs. Torrence. And what was our telephone number at the parsonage? I remember it well: two longs and a short. Mrs. Torrence answered two shorts and a long; Mrs. Webb, three longs; Doyce Ellis, a short and a long.

Then there was Mr. Wood, who wore a hearing aid and picked up the receiver on every ring, but he always got the information backwards. Mr. Wood would probably have had the Americans attacking the Japanese in a sneak attack on Tokyo Bay; Christine Holloway marrying Elvis Shurling; and C. L. Barfield going steady with Carolyn Batten. Divestiture would never have affected Mr. Wood. In fact, I doubt that he knew his own number.

But one day Mr. Wood made a near fatal mistake while listening in on a party line conversation between Mrs. Torrence and Mrs. Webb. Here's what happened.

Mrs. Webb had called Mrs. Torrence to wish her a happy birthday, and Mrs. Torrence related how it felt to be fifty-nine.

Mr. Wood couldn't contain himself, and blurted into the telephone, "What do you mean, fifty-nine? You know dern well you're sixty-six, Bessie Torrence!"

And the conversation that transpired from that point on between Mrs. Torrence and Mr. Wood came as close to an obscene telephone call as I ever heard.

Whew!

Annual Meeting Is a Dandy

I'm not real sure who organized the Dublin chapter of the Estesians, but I'm a charter member. The organization is so secret I'm not sure I should write about it. I'll know soon.

We had our annual meeting and election of officers at a banquet in June at Estes Beer and Wine. It was a gala, black tie optional affair. Just to emphasize the propriety of this erstwhile group of journalists and stringers I'll tell you this: The invitations were engraved on paper towels.

The committee on arrangements did an outstanding job again this year, securing meeting space in the back booth nearest the door leading to the restrooms.

The refreshments committee arranged for beef jerky, barbecued potato chips, and peanuts for the hors d'oeuvres, along with an occasional bag of pork skins for the picky members.

The Estesians have no set time to start the meeting.

"Whenever the beer gets cold," said one old-timer.

One new member nearly got us thrown out before the meeting got underway when she ordered a frozen strawberry daiquiri.

"We don't serve no food in here, lady," the bartender told her.

I'm not positive, but I seem to recall hearing one member say the Estesians were organized for the express purposes of preserving journalistic excellence, telling jokes, and drinking beer—not necessarily in that order.

Last month's meeting indeed served to verify that the Estesians have gotten off the ground. The problem is to get them back down. And nobody can remember who was elected to what office.

The pledges were amusing this year. "Got any hors d'oeuvres in this place?" I heard one ask Rex, the bartender.

"Not if I can help it," he said. "We try to keep them foreigners out, especially on Estesian night."

Music arranged by the entertainment committee was super. Where else are you gonna' listen to the likes of the Rovers gettin' it on with "Wasn't That a Party?"; Johnny Paycheck coming on with "Carolyn," and Wayne Kemp drawing tears with the sentimental favorite "Your Wife Is Cheatin' on Us Again"?

And I itched all over when Razzy Bailey stepped to center stage and sang "Scratch My Back." And who could ever forget the Oak Ridge Boys' heart-warming rendition of "Elvira?" Talk about a bargain! Any two for a quarter or all five for half a buck.

No doubt about it, it was a night of music and dancing. Did I say dancing? You better believe it, Fred.

I've been around the Horn a time or two and seen a few floor shows, but nothing to compare with the one provided by Rex and the Estesian dancers.

We were about an hour into the meeting and had just named the "Long-neck of the Year" when the floor show started with an announcement by the master of ceremonies, Rex, the bartender. That boy commands attention. When he speaks even E.F. Hutton listens.

The Eight-ball DeLuxe, Pac-Man, and King Tut Bowling stopped as still as a dry creek when Rex rang the bell, got everybody's attention, and shouted out the feature attraction.

"Now hear this!" he yelled. "I have an announcement to make!"

All eyes were on Rex. Anticipation ran rampant. Suds were as inactive as a broken washing machine.

"Ain't nothin' in this establishment but homosexuals and tap dancers!"

Reaction? Friend, have you ever seen forty men jump to attention and start tap dancing in unison? It was a sight to behold, forty heads bobbing and weaving, eighty arms waving, eighty feet and a crutch or two tapping out the old soft shoe. I darn near gave out of breath, but I tap danced. Oh, did I ever tap dance! I Could Have Danced All Night. That Rex will put the dancers on the floor, baby.

There's something rewarding about a group of journalists and stringers as dedicated as the Estesian Society. And boy can they dance!

Now then, if we can just figure out who was elected president of the Estesians, we'll meet again next year.

Meanwhile, Rex, keep them foreigners out of the place and the dancers on their toes. And play C-2 for me, will you? You know, just for old times sake. Use the quarter on the floor near the front door.

No Sympathy for Common Ailments

Want to get scared out of your boxers? What would you think if you went to your doctor with a runny nose, and he suggested you visit a rhinologist?

A rhinologist? Where does he practice? Grant Park Zoo? Disneyworld? How was I to know the guy is a nose specialist?

Try this one on for size. You turn in for tests. Six days later you are confronted by your consultant, the guy who puts all the test results together and gives you the final evaluation. He peers through horn-rimmed glasses and John L. Lewis eyebrows for an eternity, plus eighteen seconds, and finally says, "Well, we have determined that you have spastic colitis and . . . ."

Spastic colitis! What do you do? You panic, turn over the bed-pan, and break out in a cold sweat, gasping, "Just give it to me straight, Doc. How much time do I have?"

Spastic colitis? What he was really telling you was that you are nervous and it causes the smooth muscles in your colon to tighten up. So there you lay, foaming at the mouth, a confirmed spastic!

However, being treated by a rhinologist and having spastic coli-tis is not without advantages. At least you get sympathy from friends and neighbors. After all, who's gonna' sympathize with a nervous guy with a runny nose?

You get no sympathy with common ailments. You gotta' be fancy. How much sympathy would you get if you told a friend your blood wasn't clotting properly? Maybe a "Hmmmmm," or an "Oh, I see."

Tell him you've got agranulocytosis and he'll call Jerry Lewis to arrange a telethon, and make a donation.

Bad blood just won't get it.

Never indicate that you simply had your heartbeat checked. Come on strong. Tell the coffee table you had a ballistiocardiograph and watch their eyes bulge!

Remember how she used to churn, boil clothes in a wash pot, scrub shirts and underwear on a wash board, pick blackberries, and make homemade jelly? She never missed a chore but complained every day of an ailment that generated little sympathy. Remember?

"What's the matter, Grandma? You sick?"

"Yeah, I sure am, son."

"What's the matter?"

"Shootin' pains! I got them shootin' pains . . ."

Shootin' pains! She had 'em all her life, but I never knew what they were. Still don't.

She'd have given a week's egg money just to take one electroencephalograph. It would have provided all the ammunition she needed for church meetings and family reunions. It never happened because Dr. Cooper went no further than tongue depressor, thermometer, and stethoscope. Always gave the same diagnosis.

"Shootin' pains, Miss Jessie."

Mrs. Byrd Williamson, who lived across the street, had the same symptoms and the same doctor. She received the same examination as Grandma but came away with a different diagnosis: "That ol' mess!"

No sympathy for Mrs. Williamson. Just once, she would have settled for "shootin' pains."

But Dr. Cooper was something of a psychologist as well as a GP. He gave both Grandma and Mrs. Williamson braggin' rights. He always told Grandma that her "shootin' pains" were "acute." So, what did he do for Mrs. Williamson? He assured her that "that ol' mess," was "chronic." This was not an electroencephalograph by any means, but it produced more sympathy than gout and shingles.

*   *   *

It seems that a hypochondriac, in listing all his complaints to his doctor, added that he was also losing his hearing.

"It's getting so bad, Doc, that I can't even hear myself coughing."

The doctor scribbled off a quick prescription.

"Will this improve my hearing?" he asked.

"No," replied the doctor, "but it will make you cough much louder."

Around the Clock with an Insomniac

While insomnia is nothing to lose sleep over, it's a real eye-opener.

The word *insomnia* has always fascinated me. It sounds like it should be a little country sandwiched in between Tunisia and Algeria in northern Africa. However, it's about as frustrating a thing as can happen to a human being.

If you've ever agonized through the night with insomnia you know how it goes: hit the sack following the eleven o'clock news, fluff the pillow, douse the light and . . .

Midnight: Lids closed, eyes wide open, your heart pounding like a tom-tom to an occasional screech of a hot-rodder's tires. Loudmouth crickets and other relatives in the orthopterous family chirp in Mormon-Tabernacle-Choir unison with an occasional bass solo from a bachelor bullfrog who knows not what it means to retire at a decent hour.

A futile attempt is made to count sheep, a recommended, age-old remedy for insomnia; but, while *sheep* rhymes with *sleep,* it's no go. The sheep sleep but you don't.

2:00 A.M.: All's quiet, too quiet. You anticipate the crickets, all their relatives, and the frog, straining to hear the chirps and an occasional throaty, "Knee-deep! Knee-deep," but in vain. Not even a trickle of traffic, either, and Herman the hot-rodder has either run out of gas or warped a mag wheel. And the heartbeat has quieted down, causing you to worry that maybe you're on the way out. Things jump around in your mind that went AWOL years ago. Like, is there really life after death? Suppose I'd been born in 1827, where would I be now? Do owls really sleep with their eyes open? I wonder if God knows I can't sleep? If I worked the twelve-to-eight shift at JPS, I'd be at work now and not worrying about sleep. Is a gross 144 or 164? Who cares? Who was the National League's MVP last year? Does Gaylord Perry really throw a spitter? How rich is Ted Turner, really? Why does he keep Skip Caray? Is Hodding Carter's face really petrified?

4:00 A.M.: Halfway through the night. Guess the town's early risers, like the garbage collectors, are up and about. Probably went to bed at 9:30 and slept like a lamb. I hate people, and lambs, who sleep well when I can't. They're probably performing Beethoven's *Fifth* with the lids while dead Jack Danielses sleep eternally in the cans. Garbage can lids make more noise than crickets, bachelor frogs, bad thunder, freight cars coupling, or bedpans dropped on a tile floor in a quiet hospital room. Dern, I'm thirsty! The refrigerator and water jug inside beckons . . . Ahhhh! Like sleep, we tend to take water for granted. I don't understand how camels make it all the way across the desert. More questions in the dark: What's a four-letter word for Chinese pagoda? When will the sun eclipse again, or will it? Who cares, other than astronomers? Can dogs and cats talk to each other? Is Grizzard asleep? Doug Hall? Bucky Tarpley? What's happening at Estes?

6:00 A.M.: This is ridiculous! I can't even sleep when it's time to get up. I've completely reviewed Elizabeth Taylor's love life, Zsa Zsa Gabor's husbands (in alphabetical order), named all the dead band leaders I know, reviewed Humphrey Bogart's movies, fallen in love with Lauren Bacall again. I've envied all the people I know who can wrap Christmas packages, draw straight lines, and pour syrup without dripping it on the tablecloth.

Insomnia—it sounds contagious, doesn't it? By the way, who wakes the bugler in the morning so he can blow reveille? The baker? Bakers do rise early.

Sleeping in a Hospital Chair

Like so many of life's blessings, we tend to take sleep for granted. It's one thing to make Z's in your own bed, but it's a mattress of another color when circumstances dictate that you bed down in strange surroundings.

I have concluded that my most harrowing sleep experience came within the past month, at the old Fairview Park Hospital in Room 225. I was there because my mother had broken a hip and I slept (?) in a chair next to her bed for six nights, thereby substantiating the contention of Chauncey Depew that "next to a beautiful woman, sleep is the most beautiful thing in the world."

If you've never experienced the thrill of trying to sleep in a hospital chair, it will be difficult for you to relate to such an experience.

My first night I curled up, cat-like, in the chair and dozed at most for two hours, in ten- and fifteen-minute intervals, between temperature and blood pressure readings.

My second night was no different. Same chair, same cat-like position, and the same nurse taking "temps and pressures" every ten to fifteen minutes.

My third night was different, however. After looking around the room at beddy-by time, I decided to improvise. I would make myself a bed by utilizing the following furnishings in Room 225: one high-back straight chair, one low-back straight desk chair, and one stool, or bench-looking contraption.

I shoved the stool in front of the high-back straight chair. Then I positioned the desk chair flush up against the end of the stool. Of course, this maneuver presented one immediate problem, what with my being six feet, one inch and my creation measuring a mere five feet, two inches.

My next creation was a "pillow." I accomplished this by using two bed sheets, a towel, and my windbreaker, all rolled into a ball.

Warning: When making a makeshift pillow, be sure to place your windbreaker in such a position that the zipper is on the underside of the ball. It will prevent your having to get out of your makeshift bed, thereby knocking the bedpan to the floor and scaring the stitches out of your mother. Have you ever heard a bedpan hit a tile floor in a very quiet hospital room at midnight? Ever watched the "Gong Show"? The echoes continued well past the midnight "temp and pressure" readings, which increased considerably because of my clumsiness.

With the "pillow" properly adjusted, I tried again, but faced another problem.

The high-back straight chair seat was eighteen inches high, the little stool fourteen inches high, and the desk chair twenty-two inches and sloping.

So there I lay, my head and shoulders at eighteen inches, my back and buttocks at fourteen inches, while my legs and feet aimed toward the ceiling at the height of twenty-two inches in the only three-dimensional bed I ever tried to negotiate.

I braved the monstrosity the next night, but made adjustments. I reversed position and tried it with my head and shoulders at twenty-two inches, my back and buttocks at fourteen inches, and my legs and feet at eighteen inches. Result? The same, only the cramps shifted to different positions.

What you read next is absolutely true. I ain't proud of it, but it's true.

I felt like an idiot during the third night when the "temps and pressures" nurse inquired, "Why don't you let that high-back chair down all the way, Mr. Whaley? It makes into a cot, you know."

She then proceeded to demonstrate how to make the conversion. From the way she looked at me, I'd have had one heck of a time convincing her that I'm a college graduate. But then, how the heck was I to know the darn thing made into a cot?

At least I found the bathroom the first night. And you can take my word for it, it beats the hell out of a bedpan!

Times Have Changed

America's viewpoint has changed—drastically. Like Monday, for example, when I joined a friend for dinner. As usual, I had my *Courier Herald* in hand.

I scanned the front page and there it was, this headline, above the lead story: Shuttle's Launch Is Right on Time.

"Well, I see the spacecraft got off all right," I blurted out, expecting to alert the three front booths and my table.

"Yeah . . . pass the salt, please," my dinner companion grunted.

I figured he hadn't heard me. I repeated my scoop.

"Paper says the space shuttle got off right on time, and with the largest crew ever," I said. "The thing's 155 miles high and traveling at 17,400 miles per hour. How 'bout them astronauts?"

"Right . . . pass the pepper, please," my friend echoed.

Let's face it. Times sure have changed since I was a boy and would get up from the dinner table, leave his syrup and biscuits, and hightail it outside just to get a glimpse of an airplane.

A space shot back in those days would have shocked me out of my Fruit of the Looms and sent the town drunk to the detoxification clinic, had there been one. But back in those days they just threw drunks in the tank and left them there until Monday morning. No interviews by a psychologist; no forms to be filled out by social workers; no free clinic or Medicare. Back then detoxification was called "cold turkey." "You got yourself drunk—and you can get yourself sober" was the motto of the day.

I remember how shocked the whole town was when a pair got a divorce. Whispers invaded every conversation, and deathly silence dominated any room when one of the divorced pair entered. She was immediately branded as "that woman," and he was told "I told you so."

Today? Divorces are as common as airplane flights. Nobody pays much attention to them.

I know a couple who were married and filed for divorce before the wedding pictures returned.

The vows are the same, but the people have changed.

Time was when divorces were only granted on grounds of adultery and extreme cruelty. Now, the most popular ground for getting one is "irreconcilable differences," which means in plain street talk, "Me'n Harry just don't see eye-to-eye no more. He gets the TV and I get the house. And we draw straws for the station wagon."

No, divorces aren't a surprise any more. Neither are marriages.

Remember when boy and girl used to court for a year or two, become engaged and court for another year, and then get married?

You got 'em marryin' now before they know each other's last name. And for the darndest reasons.

"Hey! You drink light beer and smoke Salems?" he says to her in the juke joint.

"Right on!" she says.

"Good! Whaddaya' say we get married, huh?" he says.

"Might as well, I ain't lately," she agrees.

"By the way, what's y'r name?" he asks, as sort of an afterthought.

No surprises these days—and I regret that.

Time was when you wouldn't believe your eyes if you read this headline, which appeared in the *Atlanta Constitution:* Ivery Getting Drug Treatment, Paper Says. And the story began, "Former Georgia Tech running back Eddie Lee Ivery of the Green Bay Packers has checked into a drug and alcohol rehabilitation center. He has been placed on the four-week, nonfootball-illness reserve list by the Packers."

One hero shot down by drugs—but sadly, no surprise. It has become a common occurrence.

There was this headline a few days earlier: Falcon's Alfred Jenkins Out for Year. The story told us that Jenkins was suffering from a "chemical dependency."

Surprised? No, not really.

The professional teams call it a "chemical dependency" when it hits one of their stars. Were the circumstances different and if the guy with the "chemical dependency" happened to be some slob shooting it up behind a Madison Street warehouse, he'd be a "junkie."

And he wouldn't be resting in some swanky drug and alcohol rehabilitation center watching television. Nope, he'd be occupying a cell in the Laurens County Hilton—"cold turkey."

Can you imagine how you'd have felt twenty-five years ago if you read headlines that told you Stan Musial, Joe Di Maggio, Ted Williams, Johnny Unitas, Otto Graham, Bob Cousey, Bob Pettit, Johnny Mize, Bob Feller, Hal Newhouser, or Early Wynn, had a "chemical dependency"?

I think I'd have cried from the Fourth of July until Labor Day.

I don't like to admit it, but it sure looks like the pros are going to pot.

CAB's Smoke Bomb Could Backfire

The Civil Aeronautics Board (CAB) dropped a smoke bomb, voting 4–0 to propose a smoking ban on commercial flights of less than one or two hours duration.

I can foresee some problems the ban will generate. Heck, I know smokers who'd cut you for less than that. When you start messin' with smokers, you've stepped on a lot of people's filters. Some won't survive the smoking ban.

• *Smokey Harper*: Smokey lives between Cobbtown and Metter where he runs a general store and cane grinding mill. He could never survive without a cigarette for two hours—one for that matter.

Smokey is a long-time Prince Albert smoker who rolls his own. He uses OCB papers and stick matches, which he strikes on the top right gallus hook on his Dee Cee overalls. I can't recall ever seeing Smokey when he wasn't rolling, lighting, or smoking.

• *Cooter Boykin*: Cooter is from Oglethorpe where he peddles Watkins products from the back seat of a 1947 Dodge and trains bird dogs.

I've know Cooter since 1936. He used to hunt quail with my daddy. His standard equipment for a day-long hunt was five boxes of shotgun shells and five packages of Pall Malls. If he ran out of either, he quit hunting and headed home.

According to my daddy, ol' Cooter dang near died when he ran out of matches one afternoon.

"First, he cranked up my old 1934 Ford and tried to light a cigarette off the tailpipe, then the muffler, then the manifold," Daddy said. "No luck."

Completely frustrated, Cooter then searched the inside of the car from top to bottom for a match. No luck.

"Finally, he fired his 12-gauge pump at one end of a Pall Mall in desperation, blowing the cigarette to smithereens," Daddy said. "Then, he started blowing the horn, and I came from deep in the branch where I was looking for one of the dogs. I saw Cooter pacing back and forth, a cigarette hanging from his mouth, as nervous as a squirrel."

"Let's go, preacher! Got to get home, quick!" Cooter barked.

So they loaded the dogs in the trunk, unloaded their shotguns, and got in the front seat. Daddy was in the driver's seat.

"Before we drove off, Cooter, who was having a nicotine fit, watched in disbelief as I reached over, pushed in the cigarette lighter, and lit up a cigar," Daddy used to tell.

What was Cooter's reaction? One sentence, including an apology: "Well, I'll be damned! Oh, uh . . . excuse me, preacher."

• *Jake Proctor*: Jake is from Louvale, nine miles north of Lumpkin on U.S. 27 toward Columbus. He's been a civilian employee at Fort Benning since World War I.

Jake's the oldest church usher in Stewart County, and he's a smoker, a real smoker. In fact, he's been known to steal a drag or two during the Doxology, can barely make it through the offering, and prays silently every Sunday morning for a lengthy anthem and a short sermon as he fingers his trusty Zippo.

Jake's a Bugler smoker, and confirmed reports have it that in 1942 he dang near burned the church building down when he left his cigarette in a hall closet during a Christmas program in which his little granddaughter played the Virgin Mary.

• *Mrs. Nora Nelson*: Mrs. Nelson lived in a big old rambling house near Alma and raised cats. She also smoked. I mean she *really* smoked! She bought plugs of Brown's Mule, cut it into little pieces, and rolled her own in brown paper. Jack Smith and I "confiscated" one of her creations in the early 30s and crawled up under the church and smoked it. (I saw Jack last year at the Georgia–Florida game. He's still coughing.)

Warning! To the CAB and all commercial airline flights of less than two hours duration: Should you observe the name Cooter Boykin on a passenger manifest—beware! He'll hijack your airplane and force you to land in Willacoochee before he'll go two hours without a Pall Mall.

Another thing about Cooter. He'll climb out on the wing and try to light up from the flames coming out of number three engine.

Better look closely for the name Jake Proctor, too, short-trip airlines. He's serious about his smoking.

Jake'll jump!

A Good Shopper I Ain't

I'll be the first to admit that I'm the worst shopper south of Lenox Square.

In 1944 I purchased long handle underwear, wool socks, and a turtle neck sweater in preparation for my overseas assignment in the big war. Know where I debarked? In the beautiful blue waters of the Pacific, just off the shore of San Fernando, a village on the island of Luzon, just north of Manila, in the Philippine Islands. The temperature? 110 degrees.

In 1968, I was in downtown Savannah waiting to testify before a federal grand jury. I walked past what was then the Manger Hotel.

It was going out of business as the building was to be torn down, and an auction of the contents was in progress.

Want to buy a few doorknobs? A whole bunch of doorknobs? I've got 'em, because I bid on and bought 300 of the suckers for twenty-five cents each. As far as I know, they're still stored in the River Street warehouse of a friend in the port city.

I purchased a beautiful pair of light blue slacks two years ago. What a buy! A pair of $52.00-slacks for the unbelievably low price of $9.99. And, if you happen to know anybody who could use them, let me know. They're hanging in my closet. Never been worn.

What's wrong with my slacks? Nothing much, other than the fact that they have a thirty-inch waist, and I stretch the tape to a rotund thirty-five. Did I try 'em on? Naw, not me. Why haven't I returned them? Are you off your gourd? Return them and admit to the sales clerk that I made a dumb mistake? Never!

I jumped at another bargain last year at the Atlanta airport gift shop.

Are you by any chance familiar with those cute little hand puppets that do all sorts of clever tricks? Well, I invested fourteen dollars in a pair of 'em, one for each grandson. I just knew I'd tickle them pink with such an unusual remembrance.

Psssst! Wanna' buy a hand puppet? I have two that are as lifeless as King Tut—and as mute as Harpo Marx. You see, the guy who sold them to me could make them do all kinds of things: turn their cute little heads, wiggle their cute little ears, scrunch up their cute little mouths, and wink their cute little eyes while saying the cleverest little things you ever heard.

Understand me, now. I said the guy who sold them to me could make them do all those things. Me? I might as well have been trying to make an anvil perform when I stood before my audience of two, ages six and one, who stared at me like I was an idiot when I repeatedly said, "Now then, watch this."

Nothing. They saw the puppets do absolutely nothing. And how the heck was I supposed to know that a fella' had to be a ventriloquist to make the puppets talk?

I've made some other dandy purchases. Like the time in 1974 when antifreeze was in such short supply and selling for as much as eight dollars per gallon, if you were lucky enough to find any.

I really found a bargain at a Milledgeville service station where the stuff was going for $3.50 per gallon (limit two to a customer). I begged and pleaded with the owner until he finally permitted me to buy four gallons.

Know what I was driving in 1974? A Volkswagen! And even my six-year-old grandson knows that Volkswagens don't have radiators.

I also have on hand a case of Hadacol, a pair of spats, a half dozen hula hoops, two Davy Crockett coonskin caps, a Captain Marvel ring, eight "put a tiger in your tank" tails, and a Jew's harp.

The Boxer (Shorts) Rebellion

Well, well, here we are again in limbo time: the week between Christmas and New Year's.

It might best be characterized as the aftermath of the Christmas cyclone, the hallelujah hurricane, or the December dilemma.

In retrospect, I don't understand why we put ourselves through the torture that accompanies Christmas shopping. Like driving in the midst of thousands of motorized maniacs in a furious frenzy to "get there," fight for a parking place, battle through a mass of hypnotized humanity, only to divest yourself of hard-earned cash for things that normally wouldn't warrant a second look at a yard sale.

I was in Atlanta the weekend before Christmas. My hotel, the Terrace Garden Inn, is located within three "Ho! Ho! Ho!'s" of the Ninth Wonder of the World—Lenox Square. Let me tell you about shopping at Lenox Square.

In the first place, you don't "shop" Lenox Square—you survive it. And just getting inside Rich's is a masterpiece of manipulation, provided you can find a parking place. I didn't. I walked from the hotel.

I was practically assaulted trying to enter the back door of Rich's, *the* store in Atlanta.

It's a felony to go shopping in Atlanta and return without at least one Rich's shopping bag. And a fitting sentence to fit the crime would be to serve a four-hour stint in Rich's basement store. I tried it and could abide it but ten minutes.

I didn't really have anything specific in mind. I merely wanted to make a small purchase, anything that would permit me to parade around the lobby of the Terrace Garden Inn with a Rich's shopping bag in hand.

I opted for a pair of undershorts. Everybody, especially a bachelor, can always use another pair of undershorts. And I prefer boxers. Sounds like it would be easy to just walk in, buy a pair of boxer shorts, take the Rich's shopping bag, and leave, huh? I'd rather have a hemorrhoid operation or a wisdom tooth pulled than try and buy a pair of boxer shorts in Rich's basement store during Christmas.

In the first place, the clerks and mannequins all look alike, all prematurely gray at twenty-seven, and weighing eighty-three pounds. Plus, it's downright embarrassing to discuss the fine points of boxer shorts for three minutes with what you believe to be a store clerk only to learn that she is a mannequin. But it does draw a crowd, including the store detective and the mall psychiatrist.

Also I ain't particularly fond of having young ladies sell me undershorts no way.

I finally gave up on Rich's and went to a little novelty shop with blinking lights in the window and a stereo system borrowed from the Rolling Stones for the season. I forget the name, conveniently, because I really can't afford a libel suit right now.

Clothes were hanging from the ceiling and one of those "Missy Prissys," a transplanted New Jersey American no doubt, appeared before me at the undershorts counter with those "I wish I'd gone home early last night" eyes, surrounded by smeared mascara, and mumbled what sounded like, "Hoi, may oi help you?"

"Right, how much are the undershorts?" I asked. "Boxers, size 34. This pale blue pair will do."

Like a tornado, without warning, she snatched up the first pair in reach—a disgusting black pair with three-inch bright red hearts bordering the words, "I'm in the Nude for Love"—and hoisted them at arm's length above her head. Know what she did next?

She completely drowned out the Rolling Stones as she yelled at the top of her voice all the way over the bedroom shoes, bathrobes, ties, sweaters, and shaving lotion to a cute little fellow who was busily dressing a mannequin in an Izod windbreaker, scarf, and wool cap, to go skiing.

"Heeeeyyy, Jeeeerrrryyyyy!" she screeched. "This man wants to know how much these undershorts are?"

I closed my eyes as every head in the aforementioned departments, male and female, customers and clerks, grown-ups and children, snapped our way. And there stood my real live mannequin, holding aloft the most ridiculous pair of undershorts in Georgia high above her platinum head.

Me? I had but two choices: to go ahead and die or face the throng who were unanimous in their assertion that I was a dirty old man, because it was right there, in white letters inside a bright red heart—"I'm in the Nude for Love."

But my boxer (shorts) rebellion wasn't a total loss. At least Jerry appreciated it because he paused, leaving a half-naked skiier exposed to the world, winked at me, and smiled.

And I could have sworn I could read his lips as he whispered below the level of the Rolling Stones's thunder, "I love you."

I got the heck out of there, with no Rich's shopping bag and no undershorts.

Sylvia Adds Spice to Sunday Dinner

One of my greatest pleasures is having Sunday dinner with my mother. She has to be one the easiest people in the world to please. Vienna sausage, saltine crackers, and a big orange would suit the lady just fine as long as she could top off the meal with a slice of Mrs. Edwards' lemon pie.

Our Sunday routine varies little. I call about 10:00 A.M. to ask if she'd like to eat with me. The answer is always the same. "Yes, what time are you going to pick me up?" And, she's *always* ready.

Once outside the nursing home, the routine continues. "Where would you like to eat?" I ask.

"I'd like to go eat with Sylvia," she replies.

Who is Sylvia, you ask? She's a waitress, a pretty waitress, an excellent waitress.

I have this thing about waitresses. I see a lot of 'em in a year. I see good waitresses, bad waitresses, patient waitresses, and impatient waitresses. I see hash slingers and I see those who regard their profession as a challenge to serve. Theirs is not an easy job.

It must have been about six months ago that Mama and I met Sylvia. We were seated at her table by mistake. I had asked not to be seated in her station. Why? Because I'm opinionated, that's why. I simply didn't like her hairdo. Looked like she had just stuck her finger in an electrical outlet. You know, one of those curlicue hairdos resembling a frightened poodle.

We made it through the meal and the service was excellent. For the next several weeks, I took Mama to a different restaurant.

Somehow, we wound up back in the restaurant where Sylvia works for Sunday dinner. But, not in her station. I maneuvered all the way to the side and near the front, far from Sylvia's domain.

We hadn't been seated more than five minutes when I saw a waitress with *beautiful* hair come from the kitchen. I stared and stared. Finally, I asked the waitress assigned to our table if they had a new waitress, the one with the pretty hair.

"Don't you know who that is, Mr. Whaley? That's Sylvia! And, isn't her hair pretty? I just love it!" she said.

It was pretty. It was beautiful. I couldn't believe it was the same girl. I complimented her on it when she walked over to say hello to my mother.

"I've been missing you," she said.

I told her the whole story and apologized. "I'm sorry. And your hair is beautiful," I said.

We haven't missed a Sunday dinner with Sylvia since.

It happens every Sunday now. When we arrive for dinner the other waitresses steer us to Sylvia's station. I think my mother has adopted her. Maybe I have also. It's more than a meal. It's a visit with a friend.

There are many excellent places in Dublin to have Sunday dinner so it isn't the food that attracts us to the Holiday Inn. It's Sylvia. She could make cobwebs and Cool Whip taste like Mrs. Edwards' lemon pie. She's that courteous and attentive.

It was three Sundays ago when Mama and I were doing our thing at Sunday dinner. Sylvia was waiting on us. Pleasant, very pleasant. Then it happened.

Some jerk was sitting with three others at a table right next to ours. Sylvia was their waitress too.

"Listen, young lady, if my food isn't out here in five minutes, I'm leaving!" the jerk said.

I ordered a coffee refill just to wait and see what the jerk had ordered. Certainly it must have been chateaubriand or roast duck in wine sauce for him to have passed up the buffet. Maybe caviar and quail?

I listened to him chastise the waitress and low-rate the eating establishment. "Can't get no decent service any more!" he bellowed.

Then I changed my mind. Undoubtedly the jerk had ordered oats. I wondered where he'd parked the front end of the horse? As I mused his order was delivered. Chateaubriand? Roast duck? Caviar? Quail? Hardly. Sylvia placed before him a bacon, lettuce, and tomato sandwich! And she smiled.

I couldn't be a waitress.

I watched the jerk devour the sandwich in about four gulps, get up, and storm out. Tip? Perish the thought.

It brought to mind this little anecdote: The customer fumed at the waitress and publicly berated her for not having brought his order. He concluded his tirade with, "Tell me, young lady, why is it that I don't get the service I deserve in this place?"

Calmly, the waitress replied, "Possibly, sir, it's because we are too polite."

Let the Men in the Cheerleaders' Locker Rooms

Sometimes it takes forever to get my thoughts down on paper. I recently experienced one of these mental blocks when I got up at 5:33 A.M. to write National Football League commissioner Paul Tagliabue. I didn't get into the meat of it until 10:30 A.M. when I finally learned how to spell his name.

It's a difficult name to type, like President Bush's chief of staff John Sununu. Typing Sununu is like typing banana, I never know where to stop and it comes out Sununununununu . . .

I called around for help, my first call going to "Hobo" Harrison who lives alternately in Seaboard and Atlantic Coast Line boxcars. He takes calls every second Saturday between 9:30 and 10:30 A.M. at a pay phone in Waycross.

"Hello, Hobo?"

"Yeah, but hurry. Got 'nother call comin' in three minutes," he said.

"O.K., just a quick question. How do you spell Tagliabue?"

"Easy, L-A-S-H L-A-R-U-E," he said.

"No! Tagliabue, the NFL Commissioner, not Lash Larue, the western movie star!"

"They's a long freight goin' by an' it sounded like you said 'Lash Larue' or 'Taglyboo' or somethin' like that."

"I did."

"Look, I'm a busy man, an' I've got the southbound freight to catch in thirteen minutes. 'Taglyboo?' Ain't no such name," he said and hung up.

I called Robbie Nell Bell from Alma (Robbie Nail Bail fum Almer).

"Robbie Nell?"

"Hey, newspaper man! What's happenin' in civilization?"

"Not a whole lot. Just want to ask you a question . . ."

"Shoot!" she said.

"Are you familiar with Tagliabue? If so, how do you spell it?"

"Naw, not really. But I've heard of 'em," she said. "Las' year Bully Barfield an' a bunch o' fellas' went Tagliabou huntin' in Maine an' he killed one. But when time come to leave, Bully was so drunk he couldn't find th' thing."

"Not caribou! I'm talking about National Football League commissioner Paul Tagliabue!"

"Call Popeye Parker in Pembroke. He knows football," Robbie Nell allowed. "Heck, he quits his job ever September an' don't go back till after the Pro Bowl. Jus' sits in front o' his TV all day an' till late Monday nights. He'll know."

She was right . . .

"T-A-G-L-I-A-B-U-E," he said.

Then, I was ready.

Dear Mr. Tagliabue,

I've been reading about the ruckus stirred up when reporters Lisa Olson of the Boston *Herald* and Denise Tom of *USA Today* were barred from the locker rooms of the New England Patriots and the Cincinnati Bengals respectively. And your fine of $30,000 levied against Bengals coach Sam Wyche was interesting, but dumb.

I will be in Dallas in late November and plan to attend a Cowboys game, if they're still playing. And inasmuch as I presume your dictatorial authority covers every phase of the NFL, I request locker room credentials—not the players' locker room but the Dallas Cowboy cheerleaders' locker room.

You see, Tag, the way I figure it is this: by late November, every female reporter with a Bic pen and a notebook will be in the players' locker room, and standing in line to get to a Cowboy player will be worse than checking out of a supermarket. So I'm opting for the next best thing, to talk to somebody who was close to the action for details—the cheerleaders.

By the way, you are an Equal Opportunity Commissioner, aren't you, Tag?

I'll be anxiously awaiting my locker room credentials.

Yours truly,
Bo Whaley.

Storytelling in Blue Ridge Country

One of my favorite places to visit is the Blue Ridge Mountains area of North Carolina. Whenever I'm there I become convinced that God made mountains to impress on man how insignificant he is.

An artist could go bananas there. So could a writer. The scenery is breathtaking, the Biltmore House indescribable, the people friendly, the storytellers legendary. Here are three favorites I've picked up in my travels:

There was once a great snowfall in western North Carolina, and many people were snowed in for days. The Red Cross came, and two workers who heard of an old lady who lived in the mountains alone set out to find her.

After slipping and sliding in their four-wheel-drive vehicle for hours, they finally located her shack and knocked on the front door. When she came to the door, one worker said, "Hello, we're from the Red Cross—" but before she could say anything else, the lady said, "I don't believe I'm gonna' be able to help none this year. It's been a right hard winter."

An old mountaineer was walking up a mountain road and met a friend walking down, carrying a Bible.

"Where you headed?"

"Into town to catch th' bus to Cincinnati. I been hearin' 'bout them sportin' houses thar, with all them good-lookin' women. I aim to have me a good time."

"Why are you carryin' y'r Bible?"

"Well, if them sportin' houses are as interestin' as I hear tell," he said, "I might jus' stay over 'til Sunday."

Every time the man and his wife went on vacation, they boarded the cat at the "cattery." The cat got wise after a few summers, didn't like to be cooped up, and wanted to stay home.

Behind the house was a row of Lombardy poplar trees, about ten inches around and two hundred feet tall. The cat figured if he climbed far enough up in one of 'em, the man couldn't get him.

The next time the cat saw the man loading the car, he knew he was coming to get him, so he went straight to the top of a tree.

"We can't leave 'til we get that $#%& down!" the man growled.

"How?" his wife asked.

"Go to the shed and get a long rope," he said.

She did, and he climbed as far up the tree as he could, tied the rope around the trunk, then came down and tied it to the rear bumper of the car.

"I'm gonna' pull the tree over, and when it gets low enough, you grab the cat," he said.

"Okay."

He pulled ahead, looked in the rear-view mirror, and saw the tree coming down. He stopped.

"Pull up a little more!" his wife yelled.

He pulled ahead about three more feet and stopped.

"Still can't reach him!" she hollered. "About two more feet!"

As he was pulling ahead, he looked back and saw the rope beginning to fray. The tree was bent low, and the cat hadn't budged from his tree-top perch. Before the wife could grab the cat, the rope broke! The tree sprang upward, and the last they saw of the cat he was soaring high over the Lombardy poplars, spread-eagle and screeching frantically. And when he disappeared, he was still rising! They said later that the cat went over the trees, Black

Mountain, a shopping center just outside Asheville, and five city blocks!

They canceled their departure and spent the next few days looking for the cat, but couldn't find it. When the wife went to the store, she ran into a friend who lived in the next county. She was buying cat food.

"I didn't know you had a cat," she said.

"We didn't, but you know how we've been praying for one," she said. "Well, night before last, Clarence and I were charcoaling in the back yard when all of sudden this beautiful cat came falling from the sky and landed in the swimming pool. Clarence looked over at me and said, 'Hallelujah, Ethel! Our prayers have been answered! The good Lord has sent us a cat!'"

Hamburger Helper Tops This Picky Eater's List

Right out of the starting gate, let me admit that I'm a picky eater. I don't eat nothin' I don't like, can't recognize, or have difficulty pronouncing.

If I had to choose a final meal and it was possible to have it, I'd ask for roast beef and gravy, rice, little conch peas, fresh home-grown tomatoes that squirt acid when sliced, homemade biscuits with gobs of yellow cow butter, and apple-banana-raisin salad topped with chopped pecans, a big pitcher of sweetened ice tea and real ice-house ice. I'd top it all off with a big bowl of heavenly hash or ambrosia and pound cake.

All these dishes would be prepared by my mama on a wood stove, from scratch. Nothing instant, frozen, concentrated, dehydrated, or freeze-dried.

Nobody could cook roast beef, gravy, and homemade biscuits like my mama. She hasn't cooked for the past thirteen years, and I flat miss it.

The closest I come now to Mama's cooking is at Ma Hawkins Restaurant where I eat about 1,000 meals a year. Ma Hawkins comes as close to Mama's cooking as anyone, as far as my taste buds are concerned.

Now then, this may come as a surprise to everybody except my daughter, but my favorite dish is Potato Stroganoff Hamburger

Helper. What? Hamburger Helper? Yes.

I'm convinced that any spiffy restaurant could prepare a batch of Potato Stroganoff Hamburger Helper, garnish it with parsley, sprinkle shaved carrots and something red and green on it, surround it with sliced tomatoes, put it on the menu, call it "Hombuerguerre Halpeure en Casserole," price it at $19.95, and sell tons of it.

You don't think so? I have only to consider what chefs have done with swordfish that they forgot about, left on the stove unattended, and burned to a crisp. Did they throw it out? No, they simply added it to the menu as Blackened Swordfish, soaked it with Louisiana Hot Sauce, jacked the price up 200 percent, and served it to the rich and famous at Sea Island, Palm Springs, and New Orleans—the waiter explaining that it was "in vogue." They could have done the same thing with Blackened Toast, Blackened Biscuits, or Blackened Streak-O-Lean as long as the diners were convinced each was the "in" thing and imported.

About three years ago I gave my daughter twenty-four beautiful ribeye steaks when I visited her in Macon. A few weeks later she called and invited me for a "special dinner," just the two of us at her apartment. Naturally, I accepted and drove to Macon with visions of a ribeye, baked potato, homemade rolls—the works. Wrong. She topped that with what she knew was my favorite meal: Hamburger Helper. It was great!

The young lady just has a way of working hard to please her daddy, and she does.

Questions I'd Like to Ask a Talk Show Host

My lack of knowledge in certain areas surfaced several months ago while I was driving to Tallahassee, Florida, on U.S. 19 between Meigs and Ochlochnee, with a scheduled stop in nearby Thomasville. As I drove along dodging dead possums and beer cans, I listened to one of the zillions of talk shows that dominate radio. Talk shows keep me awake anticipating the next stupid question and the next stupid answer. The one I was listening to was one on which the host was a psychologist, the bottom of the talk show barrel.

Talk show host psychologists know everything from how to burp a baby to how to get squirrels out of the attic. Put a psychologist on a talk show, and it makes my forefinger twitch wanting to stop at a pay phone and call in. And they all—male and female—automatically become comedians when the microphone is turned on.

I truly wanted to stop and call the 800 number that was repeated every fourteen seconds and pop a question or two. I didn't, but here are some that I would have posed to Dr. Dum Dum had I done so. I know you know the answers. I don't.

- What's the difference between beer and ale?
- What is *perestroika* as opposed to *glasnost*?
- What's the difference between a petit and a traverse jury?
- What's the difference between habeas corpus and corpus delecti?
- What's the difference between a speedometer and an odometer?
- What's the difference between rayon, nylon, and dacron?
- What's the difference between a first cousin and a second cousin once removed?
- What's the difference between a bagel, a bugle, and a beagle?
- What does *AM* and *FM* stand for in radio?
- What does *WD* stand for in WD-40? And is there a WD-30? Or WD-50?
- What does *STP* stand for?
- What's the difference between Fahrenheit and Celsius?
- What's the difference between an unabridged and an abridged dictionary?
- When being afforded a physical exam and the doctor orders you to "strip to the waist," should you remove your shirt or trousers?
- What does the term *bare facts* mean to a nudist?
- What's the difference between fluorescent, incandescent, and iridescent lighting?
- Surely you are familiar with dry cell batteries, but are there any wet cell ones?
- Which sex is the opposite sex?
- When does a kitten become a cat? Or a puppy a dog?

Part 7

Six Favorite Columns

It has been my privilege to write over 1,400 columns for the *Courier Herald* as of this publication. Each contains an integral part of me.

But columns are a lot like fresh milk: Let them sit for a while and the cream will come to the top.

Here, then, is the cream.

Her Faith Lasted Through Hard Times

THIS STORY HAS BEEN on the tips of my fingers for more than a year.

It's the story of a girl; a story of perseverance, dedication, and priorities; a story of highs and lows, exhilaration and disappointment, dreams and nightmares. But more than that, it's a story of clinging to a strong faith in God, loyalty to a church that nursed her through trials and tribulations, and it's a story of emotional survival.

This, then, is the story of Martha (not her real name).

Martha is young and beautiful with a radiant smile, dancing eyes, and a faith in God that is boundless.

She has seen, and coped with, more problems than a math teacher, more heartaches than an electrocardiograph, more disappointments than a compulsive gambler. But you'd never learn that from her. It just isn't her nature to complain and moan that "fate has dealt me a bad hand."

What girl doesn't dream of being a high school honor graduate, finishing college, marrying her high school sweetheart in a June wedding, and having children? Not only did Martha dream about all these things, her dreams came true and her world was as beautiful as she. The American dream—she was living it.

But suddenly, and without warning, the grim hand of fate reached out and struck its initial blow. The dream ended and her nightmare began.

Her child, an eighteen-month-old daughter, died suddenly in the fourth year of her marriage. A year and a half later she gave birth to another.

Meanwhile, in the eighth year of her marriage, what had begun as the dream marriage began to crumble. There was a separation, then another, and yet another, until, finally, the inevitable—divorce.

Martha was left to fight the world with a two-year-old soldier and very little ammunition. Understandably, she could have thrown up her hands in despair and cried out, "Why me, Lord?" but she didn't. She could have run away from her responsibilities but she didn't. She could have become bitter and withdrawn, but she didn't.

Instead, she reached out, calling on a strong faith in God, and found added strength in a loving and compassionate church that helped her cope with her frustrations and responsibilities.

Somehow she survived the turmoil and turbulence that come with having no husband, no job, and a two-year-old looking to mama for help in becoming three.

It reached the point where dollars, as scarce as hens' teeth, looked as big as bed sheets. Part-time jobs came and went: a seemingly endless cycle of applications, interviews, and terminations, a revolving door with no exit. But she hung on, disappointed but not disgusted; concerned but not compulsive; fearful but not frantic.

Through it all, she stuck by her church, loyal in attendance while giving what she could, the widow's mite, primarily her limited talents on the organ and piano. This is what brought her to my attention.

After what seemed like hundreds of fruitless applications and interviews in search of a regular job, she finally struck paydirt.

She made application along with 200 others, was interviewed, and hired. The sun came out, a little.

Hers wasn't the highest paying job around, but it was a job and a regular paycheck. The worm had turned, a little.

So, what's so special about Martha, you ask? Many young women are divorced, having children to raise, and find it rough making ends meet.

What impressed me so much about Martha was what she did with her money once she began working regularly. To her, it was simply a matter of priorities.

New dress? Jewelry? A night out? No, none of these.

With one of her first paychecks she did something she had wanted to do for so long. She bought some flowers for her little girl's grave. And I watched her place them there.

Her next move was to contact a music teacher and arrange to take organ lessons, not every week, but every other week. Priorities, friends. It's called priorities.

"I'm very limited on the organ and I feel I owe it to my church to learn to play as well as I can. My church stood by me when I needed it most, giving me love, concern, and tremendous emotional support. I'll never forget that," she said. "I guess I'm just trying to repay with music what they gave me through prayer and love."

With Martha, life is a matter of priorities, and she has hers in good order. Her commitment to a dead child and a living church are strong indications of that.

Wouldn't any church be fortunate to have her as a member? Or any child for a mother? Or any man for a wife?

I think so.

He Does Work in Mysterious Ways

Jason Hutcheson was sixteen when he died in a tragic traffic accident, and the young Eagle Scout truly lived a full and meaningful life right up to the end. Written evidence of this was provided to me recently by his father.

On a recent evening, James Hutcheson was at home alone. He reached for the family Bible and read what has to be the most meaningful epistle he's ever read in that great book. And it wasn't written by Matthew, Mark, Luke, or John—but by Jason, his son. This is what James read, with understandable pride:

> I am Jason Hutcheson, the son of James Hutcheson, and because I am my father's son I can expect to receive certain things from him.
>
> If I am a good and obedient son I can expect my father to love me, to help me, to provide for me, and ultimately allow me to share in whatever material things he has. My happiness and well-being are of the utmost importance to my father and I am one of the most valuable things in his life.
>
> In this regard, I want you to read Romans 8:14–17, for that passage of Scripture tells about my other father:
>
> "For as many as are led by the Spirit of God, they are the sons of God. 15 . . . For ye have not received the spirit of bondage again to fear; but ye have received the Spirit of adoption, whereby we cry, Abba, Father. 16 . . . The Spirit itself beareth witness with our spirit, that we are the children of God: 17 . . . And if children, then heirs; heirs of God, and joint-heirs with Christ; if so be that we suffer with Him, that we may also be glorified together."
>
> According to these verses, if I am a good and obedient son, my heavenly Father will acknowledge me as His son. His spirit will speak to my spirit and will assure me that our Father-son relationship is secure and that I am a joint heir to His kingdom with His other son, Jesus.
>
> This means that the God that created the universe and all that is in it is ready, willing, and able to do good things for me beyond my ability to imagine or even want. It means that I am nobility—a child of the King.
>
> It means that my safety is assured, my well-being guaranteed, and that I should be unafraid for He is always with me.
>
> My heavenly Father owns the wealth of the world and He has promised to do good things for me all the days of my life and that I will live in His house forever. He has even sent His own son, Jesus, to build me a mansion in glory and some day I'll move there and live with Him in perfect peace and happiness.
>
> Sometimes, earthly fathers aren't able to supply their children with all of the things that they would like for them to have, but my heavenly Father will always be God and His kingdom will never diminish—not even after the world is no more.
>
> I'm proud of my earthly father, and I'm grateful for his love and all the things that he does for me, but I'm even more pleased to be a

child of the King and a joint heir to his kingdom with his other son, Jesus.

James Hutcheson found this in the family Bible. Something beyond our comprehension prompted him to reach for it, open it, and read. He found a bonus in the family Bible.

After having read Jason's writing, I recalled something I'd seen many years ago, an explanation of what the Bible really is. I've saved it for a special occasion and this is where it belongs, in light of Jason's message.

Many truthful and important things may be said and written about the Bible but I know of none that expresses more beautifully and fully what this great Book is than this:

> The Bible contains the mind of God, the state of man, the way of salvation, the doom of sinners, and the happiness of believers. Its doctrines are holy, its precepts are binding, its histories are true, and its decisions are indisputable. Read it to be wise, believe it to be safe, and practice it to be holy.

> The Bible contains light to direct you, food to support you, and comfort to cheer you. It is the traveler's map, the pilgrim's staff, the pilot's compass, the soldier's sword, and the Christian's charter.

> Inside it, Paradise is restored, Heaven is opened, and Hell is disclosed. Christ is its grand object, our good is its design, and the glory of God its end. It should fill the memory, rule the heart, and guide the feet.

> Read it slowly, frequently, and prayerfully for it is a mine of wealth, a paradise of glory, and a river of pleasure. It is given you in life, will be opened in judgment, and remembered forever.

> It involves the greatest responsibility, will reward the highest labor, and will condemn all who dare to trifle with its sacred contents.

> It offers protection for infancy, happiness for childhood, inspiration for youth, strength for maturity, assurance for old age, comfort for death, and salvation and riches and glory and reward for eternity.

The Bible is filled with riches untold—but you must reach for it, open it, and read it in order to find them. None appear on the cover.

Does Prayer Cause Things to Happen?

My preacher prefaced his Sunday morning prayer with this observation: "Prayer just causes things to happen. I'm convinced of it." Then he led us in prayer.

I considered his preface to prayer carefully and reached for the pew Bible in front of me. I found the passage of Scripture his words brought to mind, Matthew 7:7, undoubtedly familiar to many of you: "Ask, and it shall be given you; seek, and ye shall find; knock, and it shall be opened unto you." These words of Jesus are directions concerning prayer given to his disciples in the Sermon on the Mount.

The three key words are: ask, seek, and knock. Each denotes action, action that must be initiated to cause things to happen.

Does prayer really cause things to happen? Please read on.

It was early December 1979. I was seated at my desk when the phone rang shortly after 8:00 A.M. Our conversation was brief.

"Bo, I'd like to ask you to meet me in the chapel at Laurens Memorial Hospital. My grandbaby is real sick. It looks like the little fella's not gonna' make it. The doctor says fifty-fifty at best," he said.

"I'll be right there," I assured him.

He and his wife were already there when I arrived. His face was torn with grief and concern. His wife stared at the door. Their grandson, only four days old, had serious respiratory problems. His lungs wouldn't inflate and a respirator was keeping him alive.

"Thank you for coming. The preacher will be here any minute. He's en route from Waycross. I wanted you here to pray with us," he said.

In a matter of minutes the preacher arrived. I closed the chapel door and the four of us knelt and prayed. We prayed for a little baby boy named Curtis.

The preacher went back to Waycross. I shook the hand of a heavy-hearted grandfather, hugged the grandmother, and came back to my desk. It was a long day.

Next morning, bright and early, my telephone rang again. The same grandfather was on the line. He was jubilant, overjoyed.

"Bo, it's a miracle! I'm at the hospital and the doctor says the little fella' has a good chance to live. His lungs have filled up and he's breathing on his own. It has to be a miracle," he said. "I can't thank you enough for coming yesterday to be with us."

Thank me? No, I think not. Let me thank him for calling me. The fact that he asked me to come and pray with him may be the greatest compliment he could pay me.

That was a year ago. I talked to the grandmother last week and asked her about little Curtis.

"Oh, I wish you could see him! He's a regular butterball and so full of life. He's healthy as can be and we're so thankful," she said.

Does prayer cause things to happen? Ask Tish and Jewel Holton. They have some definite thoughts on the subject.

Beauty Is Only Skin Deep

It must have been close to 5:30 P.M. as I cruised along on I-75 South, radio on, listening to WRNG and Ludlow Porch, a funny man.

I always stop for coffee in Forsyth. I pulled off I-75, parked at the coffee shop, bought a newspaper, and settled down for a little reading and resting.

Try as I would to read my newspaper, it was useless. The girl was one of those rare beauties that make you keep reading the same paragraph over and over, sweeten your coffee twice, and put the spoon in your water glass.

She was joined shortly by a young man. They made a handsome couple. Both ordered Cokes and I heard him call her name—Linda. They sipped and chatted. I read and peeped, periodically stealing a glance to confirm that Linda was as pretty as the last time I looked. She was.

I read the first paragraph of a front page story about the Great Britain-Falklands confrontation three times and they were still involved in a bitter dispute the third time around.

I flipped to the sports page where the Atlanta Braves defeated the San Diego Padres three times in four minutes. And they would have defeated them a fourth had my attention not been diverted to the coffee shop entrance and an elderly man and woman attempting to enter, no easy task for them.

The man held the door open while the woman, obviously his wife of many years, attempted the narrow entrance. Once inside, the man helped her to a seat in the first available booth. She was physically exhausted from the short walk.

The woman's legs were wrapped with elastic bandages and both ankles were swollen twice their normal size.

The man wore a brace on his right leg and a shoe on his right foot with about a four-inch built-up sole and heel. And his hands shook a lot.

I heard enough of their conversation to determine they were from Michigan, and returning there from Florida. They had no doubt made the trip many times in past years and both were most likely in their 80s.

After they were seated, I returned my attention to the Great Britain-Falklands fiasco on page one. They were still in a turmoil.

My concentration was broken by the sound of a woman crying.

"But . . . I'm just such a . . . a burden to you . . . I'm no good for . . . anything any more . . . and I know this is . . . this is . . . our last trip to Florida," she sobbed.

Her husband tried to console her but to no avail. She continued crying and they left without ordering, struggling back to their automobile. It was quite an effort for the woman but she finally made it with the help of her husband and a walker.

I watched them drive away. She was still crying—and probably would most of the way to Michigan.

Meanwhile, Linda and her friend had finished their Cokes. She was in a giddy mood.

"But . . . I'm just such a . . . a burden to you . . . I'm just not good for anything any more," she mocked.

I watched her get up and limp toward the entrance, pretending to use an aluminum walker. I watched her as she stood there waiting for her companion to pay the check.

I watched her complexion change from silky smooth to a blotch of acne; her mascara and eye shadow run like a gutter spout; her hair become tangled and dirty and her lipstick smear all the way to her ears. And her smile had turned to a leer.

Suddenly, Linda wasn't pretty any more.

When Christmas Comes in January

A glance around the den reveals Christmas cards stacked neatly under the end table next to the picture you took with your "open me first" camera. The sight of the cards decides your evening: time to pull up a chair, relax, and review them, taking time to carefully read the verse again that was selected with such care, just for you. So you begin.

Some fifteen minutes have passed and all is well—reflections, good friends, loved ones, memories. And then you open the card signed only "Bob and Alice." You have read it nine times since it arrived and the same question arises: Who the heck are Bob and Alice?

I had my Christmas in January last night as I sprawled in front of the fireplace, with Johnny Mathis, Barbra Streisand, and Roy Clark to keep my company.

As I browsed and mentally visited friends from Texas to Michigan, from Las Vegas to New York, I picked up *the* card, which is a little different from Bob and Alice's, for I know the identity of the sender well.

It bears a postmark from Hallsboro, North Carolina, comes every Christmas, always with a little note and a small snapshot, and is signed "Winnie." This one is the fifth since Christmas, 1973.

This card has become real special to me and I would like to share with you how I came to be included on her Christmas card list. I love the story, because it is true and has such a happy ending, the best kind.

It was late, approaching midnight, as I drove toward Savannah from Jacksonville in June 1973. The rain beat hard against the windshield as the wipers struggled in vain to keep up. I pulled off Highway 17 into a service station, joining eight or ten others who had surrrendered to Mother Nature.

Once inside the station, I joined them in a cup of machine-dispensed coffee and a cold and stale ham sandwich, the greater portion of which was eventually devoured by a wet dog, the station attendant's companion. I bought it to satisfy my conscience and not just stand and drip on the floor and make use of the restroom for free.

While partaking of the coffee and chatting idly with a fellow refugee from Michigan, I saw her pull in and get out of an old, battered Chevrolet. Instinctively, I noticed the license plate: North Carolina.

When she entered the station she was holding a small piggy bank and appeared very tired and road-weary. Her long, blond hair was in tangles, her white pedal-pushers somewhat soiled, and she was barefooted. She was young, very pretty, with big brown eyes and fair complexion. Somehow, she just didn't fit the old car or the locale this dreary night.

The rain stopped shortly and all had continued on their way leaving the girl, myself, the station attendant, and the dog. I listened as she related her story to Jack.

She left home in North Carolina with no notification to her parents and drove to Fort Lauderdale to marry a boy from her home town. It hadn't worked out and she found herself stranded in Florida with an old car and no money, other than the coins in her piggy bank. She was trying to get back home but was either too proud or too ashamed, maybe both, to call home for help.

As she counted out the contents of her bank for gas, she told Jack that she was going to drive as far as she could toward North Carolina until her gas ran out, then try and work at something for a few days to get some money to go on home.

She ate heartily on the two sandwiches that Jack had given her, continuing to talk as she ate. I heard her say that she was nineteen; Jack was at least fifty-five. She counted out less than $3.00 in change and gave it to him for gas. She was receiving his full attention and I heard him make his pitch.

He had a trailer in back of the station and lived alone. Why didn't she stay overnight there until he got off work the next morning at 7:00? (It was somewhat obvious that he would have liked it very much if I left.)

He was glowing as he went outside to put the gas in her car, and I'm sure that had he had a villain's moustache he would have twisted the ends in anticipation.

Now there were three—the girl, me, and the dog. She told me her name was Winnie and that she was scared. She was considering Jack's offer; otherwise she would sleep in her car at some roadside park further up the road. She asked my opinion and I gave it: neither.

Jack could hardly take care of the other cars that were stopping as he kept his eyes fixed on the girl. I bought her another sandwich. She ate it quickly. The dog displayed no interest. I watched her as she ate. My mind's eye made a quick trip 150 miles away as I transposed the image of my teen-aged daughter, with long, blonde hair, to the station and saw her standing there, barefooted, in Winnie's place.

I reached in my pocket and took out a twenty-dollar bill. I rolled it into a tight roll and handed it to her. I told her to take a father's advice and head straight home to North Carolina and assured her that she would be welcomed back there with open arms.

Without waiting for any comment, I walked into the restroom and washed my hands. Maybe they needed it; maybe they didn't. At any rate, when I came out she was gone, and a confused and obviously disappointed Jack was standing by the doorway fingering a small and I'm sure, inexpensive ring.

"The girl said for me to give you this and to thank you. She said it was all she had," he said.

I left a baffled Jack and a sleeping dog and drove north on U.S. 17 to Interstate 95. It had started to rain again. I caught up with her old Chevy, waving for her to stop. She did, after about a mile of waving, horn-blowing, and light-blinking. I walked back to her car and handed her the ring, her birthstone, I learned. "I don't want your ring, honey. I just want you to get on home safely," I assured her.

She asked for my name and address. I gave it to her. She cried a little. (So did I.)

In about a week or ten days I received a beautiful note from her father, enclosing twenty dollars. I will cherish it always because a few months later I received a note from Winnie. Her father had died.

What has happened to Winnie? Like I promised, a happy ending. The Christmas cards started arriving in 1973 and she never misses.

She is happily married, has two fine children, a fine husband, and is living in North Carolina.

Christmas in January—it was good.

Beauty and the Beach Go Together

Socrates defined beauty as a short-lived tyranny; Plato called it a privilege of nature; Theocritus, a delightful prejudice.

Sir Francis Bacon wrote that "the best part of beauty is that which no picture can express."

And then, there was Confucius who said, "Everything has its beauty but not everyone sees it."

I wish these learned scholars could have been with me on a recent visit to Jekyll Island. Some beauty is so infinite that words are inadequate to capture and preserve it. Such was the case at Jekyll Island.

I arose very early. The sun had preceded me but a few minutes and was not yet at full glow as it peeped over the Atlantic. Its rays danced a rumba to the steady beat of roaring waves.

Walking shirtless and barefooted the hundred or so yards to the rim of the ocean, I understood the vastness and infinity of nature. Thousands upon thousands of footprints, large and small, dotted the sandy path, some going to and some coming from the salty basin.

Once seated on the beach, I became aware that I was alone. A hugh ship dotted the horizon. It was impossible to determine if it was going or coming. Its gigantic dimensions were reduced to microscopic proportions when compared to the impatient Atlantic on which it sailed. And I listened. Yes, oceans do roar.

Ignoring the vastness of the ocean for the moment, I cast my eyes upward as I sat in the sand, spent waves teasing my toes. A lone cloud hovered and sauntered about the heaven, carefree and lazy. It was billowy, bright, towering, shimmering, and fluffy—like a just bathed poodle or cotton candy. It fascinated me. And then, it was gone, on to where clouds go, on and on . . .

Socrates was right.

Deserted by the cloud, I returned my attention to the ocean. It was my turn to tease the spent waves and whitecaps as they tiptoed softly to shore and expired. But not before I teased them with my toes.

One took me seriously and slipped up on my blind side as my attention was temporarily diverted back to the sky and another cloud. It attacked and wet my bottom almost as if to say, "Gotcha."

I decided to walk along the beach, why I don't know. One mile of beach is like any other mile of beach. But there's just something about walking on a beach, and it's a good way to dry your britches.

An impatient breeze caressed my face and held my hand. Alone? I think not. The beauties of nature surrounded me. It was good to be alive.

Plato was right.

Having dined heartily on such delicacies as cotton candy clouds, salt water whitecaps, and seabreezes, I retraced my steps in the sand to my motel room to change to dry britches, don shoes and shirt, and treat myself to Sunday morning breakfast. With me it isn't a meal, it's a ritual—a bonus for having survived the night.

Little did I know that I would view the most beautiful sight on Jekyll Island as I shuffled along to the motel restaurant, stopping en route to purchase what for me is a breakfast must, a newspaper.

Inside the restaurant, the smell of fresh-brewed coffee ignited my already gigantic appetite. The anticipation of soft scrambled eggs, sausage, grits, biscuits, grapefruit, and an hour or more with my paper provided additional fuel for a fiery appetite.

I was well into my second cup of coffee and partially finished with my sausage and eggs, when he came in. He was a giant of a man, wearing a black T-shirt with a motorcycle emblem embalzoned across the chest, a massive chest. His biceps strained for freedom, testing every stitch. Immediately, I recognized two areas of common interest with the man, motorcycles and newspapers. He had one tucked under his arm as he walked to his table. (What? A motorcycle or a newspaper, you ask? Friend, the man could have had one of each. He was that big!)

With a terrific breakfast under my belt, I gave full attention to my newspaper and the remaining half cup of coffee.

From a nearby table I heard the last words of a conversation, an obvious reference to my friend in the motorcycle T-shirt.

"Oh, he's just one of them motorcycle bums."

I was finishing with breakfast and nearing the end of the final section of my paper when they came in, a beautiful lady and a little girl, maybe five, six at most. Both were wearing beach outfits and gorgeous suntans.

I had something in common with the child. She had a wet bottom. I soon learned that she'd been to my ocean for a prebreakfast swim. I wondered if she might have seen my cloud. Both lady and child were happy and giggling.

They already had a table. The lady's husband, and the little girl's father, was seated at it. Right, the man in the motorcycle T-shirt. You know, "one of them motorcycle bums."

He rose, helped his wife with her chair and patted the child on her fanny, a privilege reserved for daddies, before lifting her to her chair.

"Have a good swim?" he asked.

"Beautiful! Absolutely beautiful," the wife answered.

The child was as fresh as clean linen and as cute as the little girl in the Coppertone ad, complete with pony tail. The only thing missing was the determined Scottie tugging at her shorts, partially revealing her just-patted fanny.

I folded my paper and watched. The three of them glowed in the joy of each other's company as they made small talk and the "motorcycle bum," explained in detail a small shell found and prized by his daughter. She gave it to him and he kissed her on the forehead. She giggled. Her mother smiled.

Sir Francis Bacon? Obviously a wise man, and he was right.

Their breakfast arrived and I viewed a beautiful sight in the motel restaurant.

Obviously the child was well trained. She knew exactly what to do with her napkin, knife, fork, spoon *and* hands. Just as naturally as breathing, she bowed her head and reached right and left with them—right to daddy and left to mommy. Her pony tail lay as still as a weeping willow on a calm day.

The motorcycle bum? He offered a prayer of thanks for his family and the food before them.

The guy who had labeled the little girl's father, "just one of them motorcycle bums," had left. I wished he hadn't. I would have given my breakfast and newspaper for him to have been there.

Confucius? You be the judge.

As for me, I just have the feeling that I witnessed the most beautiful sight on Jekyll Island that Sunday morning in a busy motel restaurant.

I gathered my newspaper, paid my check, and headed back to Room 516. En route, I met a friend.

"Boy, you're up and at 'em early this morning! Going to church?" he inquired.

"Already been," I replied.

I went on upstairs, opened the door, and walked into my room. I tossed the paper in the general direction of my wet britches, opened my brief case, took out a few sheets of copy paper, and faced my typewriter.

What you just finished reading is what I wrote that Sunday morning. Like I said, words are inadequate to capture and preserve what I witnessed in that motel restaurant. But I can assure you it was beautiful.

Did I really go to church? I have to think so.

Part 8

America—Love It Or Leave It

I choke up when the American flag goes by in a parade. I sing *all* the words to the "Star Spangled Banner" at ball games and ceremonies. I cry when I hear Elvis Presley sing "The Trilogy."

And I chomp at the bit, get fighting mad, and want to run out and smack a Communist in the mouth when I hear Merle Haggard sing "The Fightin' Side of Me."

I'll take America every time. It may not be perfect, but compared to any other country I know about, it's way ahead.

The way I see it—"God Bless America, Land That I Love . . ."

"Sick" American Speaks Out on America's Ills

THERE ARE THOSE who claim ours is a "sick" society, that our country is sick, that we are sick. Well, maybe they're right. I submit that I'm sick, and maybe you are, too.

Yes, I'm sick.

• I'm sick of having policemen ridiculed and called "pigs" while cop killers are hailed by some as a sort of folk hero.

• I'm sick of being told that religion is the opiate of the people, but marijuana should be legalized.

• I'm sick of commentators and columnists canonizing anarchists, revolutionaries, and criminal rapists, but condemning law enforcement when such criminals are brought to justice.

• I'm sick of being told that pornography is the right of the free press, but freedom of the press does not include being able to read the Bible on school grounds.

• I'm sick and tired of paying more and more taxes to build more and more schools when I see some faculty members encouraging students to tear them down or burn them.

• I'm sick of Supreme Court decisions which, because of some infinitesimal technicality, turn criminals loose on society—while other decisions by this august body take away my means of protecting my home and family.

• I'm sick of pot-smoking entertainers deluging me with their condemnation of my moral standards on late-night television, moral standards which I steadfastly refuse to compromise.

• I'm sick of being told that policemen are mad dogs who should not have guns—but that criminals who use guns to maim, rob, and murder should be coddled, understood, and helped back to society, with no consideration for their victims.

• I'm sick of being told it is wrong to use napalm to end a war overseas; but if it's a Molotov cocktail or a homemade bomb at home, I'm asked to understand the provocations.

• I'm sick of not being able to take my family to a movie unless I am willing to have them exposed to nudity, homosexuality, vulgar language, and the glorification of narcotics and adultery.

And also:

• I'm sick of riots, marches, protests, demonstrations, confrontations, and the other mob temper tantrums of people intellectually incapable of working within the system.

• I'm sick of hearing the same slick slogans, the cries of people who repeatedly chant the same thing, like zombies, because they haven't the capacity of verbalizing thought.

• I'm sick of those who repeatedly say I owe them this or that because of the sins of my forefathers—when I have looked down both ends of a gun barrel to defend their rights, their liberties, and their families and would do it again without hesitation.

• I'm sick of cynical attitudes toward patriotism and equally sick of politicians with no backbone.

• I'm sick of permissiveness.

• I'm sick of the dirty, the foul-mouthed, the unwashed.

• I'm sick of the decline of personal honesty, personal integrity, and human sincerity.

*   *   *

Most of all, I'm sick of being told I'm sick by people sicker than I am. And I'm also sick of being told my country is sick—when we have the greatest nation that man has ever brought forth on the face of the earth, when fully 50 percent of the world's population would willingly trade places with the most deprived and underprivileged among us in America.

Yes, I may be sick. But if I am only sick I can get well, help my society get well, and help my country get well.

Take note, all of you. You will not find me throwing a Molotov cocktail or a bomb; you will not find me perched under a placard; you will not see me take to the streets; you will not find me ranting to the cheers of wild-eyed mobs.

No, but you will find me at work, paying taxes, supporting my family, and serving the community in which I live.

You will also find me expressing my anger and indignation to elected officials if my conscience so dictates because, you see, I'm no patsy.

You will find me speaking out in support of those officials, institutions, and personalities who contribute to the elevation of society and not to its destruction.

And you will find me contributing my time, money, and personal influence to helping churches, hospitals, deserving charities, and other establishments which have shown the true spirit of this country's determination to ease pain and suffering, eliminate hunger, and generate brotherhood.

But most of all, you'll find me at the polling place because there, if you'll listen, you can hear the thunder of the common man. There, in privacy, each of us can cast a vote for an America where people can walk the streets, day or night, without fear.

Yes, I'm sick. But I take great consolation in the knowledge that there is a cure: regular doses of prayer, patriotism, and patience.

America the Unbeautiful: It's Definitely Time for a Change

I'm a little tired this morning, having spent most of last night sitting with a sick friend. So if my paragraphs aren't balanced, my *t*'s and *i*'s incomplete, and some of my sentences run together, I beg your indulgence.

I heard a man talking about my friend at lunch yesterday. I became concerned about her so I stayed up with her most of the night.

My ailing friend is a fine lady and somewhat elderly. She celebrated her 204th birthday last month. Perhaps you know her. Her name is America. A song writer has called her beautiful.

The lady hasn't been well for some time, her illness generally diagnosed as acute recession. Some specialists say she could develop deep depression if her condition is neglected. I hope not, for her sake and ours. She went through a bad siege of that fifty years ago. In fact, she almost died in October, 1929. Many gave up on her then. Strong lady that she is, she recovered.

America has been failing with alarming rapidity in recent months. Transfusions have been ineffective and recently major surgery, a tax cut, has been prescribed. Leading tax surgeons disagree, feeling she might not survive the operation, a prime consideration for a lady of 204.

At present she's in intensive care and holding her own but inflation, the economy, and mountain-high interest rates, coupled with record unemployment, have taken their toll. I pray some irresponsible attendant doesn't pull the plug.

So what keeps her going? A strong Constitution, the strongest in the history of the world. Thank God for that.

America has indeed had her share of ailments down through the years, one of her more serious attacks coming in 1972-73. We now know it as Watergateitis. It hit her just as she appeared to be recovering from the Vietnam epidemic.

Then there was the Agnew virus followed by the Hays and Mills infections plus the Diggs and Flood plague. The sores from these had barely healed when the Abscam mess hit her. Lord! How much can a 204-year-old lady take? After all, hasn't she had Iranian cancer, recurring riot fever, Nixon nausea, and shrinkage of her dollar? Not to mention that her energy is fast being drained.

Yesterday I sat in a restaurant listening to a quack diagnose America's illness.

"You want to know what's wrong with America? I'll tell you exactly what's wrong. We're going straight to hell because of greedy, crooked politicians and a do-nothing president!"

He then proceeded to list the symptoms. Unemployment, welfare, inflation, drugs, apathy, the Congress, the high cost of living, and on and on.

Why do I peg the guy a quack? Because not once did he pre-
scribe any treatment. Legitimate doctors don't treat symptoms;
they search for, identify, and treat causes.

What's wrong with America? If I'd had a hand mirror I'd have
shown him.

Don't tell me what's wrong with America! Tell me what's right
about her! Should I dwell on her weaknesses and shortcomings I
might well be found wanting. I might be the cause instead of a
symptom. After all, what have I *really* done for her lately?

So I'm sitting up with my sick friend because the quack's comments concerned me. I wish she could talk to me. She'd probably
offer some of the wisdom that's made her so great and durable.
After all, she didn't attain the age of 204 through weakness and
cowardice, but rather through dedication and determination.

If America could talk to me, I think she would probably tell me
this:

> There are so many ready and anxious to blame my illness on the
> president and this shouldn't be. I'm above the fallacies and failures
> of any single individual, no matter what his station. My system
> assures this, so any such theory should be quickly discounted.
>
> True, the president is the chief physician but what of his
> interns—the House and the Senate, the Cabinet, department heads,
> state, county, and city officials? Are they not qualified and licensed
> to practice? No, don't blame the president alone.

The cure for what ails America is a revolution. A revolution?
Right, a revolution. In the past 200 years America has seen many
come and go. What the heck, she was born of one in 1776, wasn't
she?

The one that almost killed her came in 1861. She was a mere
child of eighty-five then. Bedridden for four years, she showed
some sign of recovery in 1865. Historians recorded it as the Civil
War. America still has her scars. Andersonville is one, a big ugly
one.

Another revolution? It's a must if America is to recover. We
must have one that recedes, takes us back to where we began when
my friend was born.

We need a moral revolution, and need it desperately.

We must recede to the point where men once again do right
because it is right and not because of a statute or ordinance that
dictates they must.

Once again we must feel the satisfaction of knowing a handshake is a contract; a promise is a covenant; a man's word is his bond.

We must recede to the day when hard work and pride in accomplishment replace greed and cunning schemes to obtain something for nothing.

We must learn again to respect dutiful labor and see it rewarded in true measure.

Finally, we must go back and rebuild the foundation of the United States of America that is fast decaying. America's foundation must be based on her faith in God. This must be the goal of each of her children if we are to endure.

I wondered as I sat with this sick lady if she would like me to read to her? If so, I would have read several of her favorites, some from her childhood. Want to see a few excerpts?

"We the people of the United States, in order to form a more perfect Union, establish Justice, insure domestic Tranquility, provide for the common Defense, promote the general Welfare, and secure the Blessing of Liberty to ourselves and our Posterity, do ordain and establish this Constitution for the United States of America . . ."

(She would have remembered this well. She was but a young girl of thirteen when it was adopted in North Carolina in 1789.)

". . . A new nation, conceived in liberty and dedicated to the proposition that all men are created equal."

". . . That this nation, under God, shall have a new birth of freedom—and that government of the people, by the people, for the people shall not perish from the earth."

"Let me first assert my firm belief that the only thing we have to fear is fear itself . . . nameless, unreasoning, unjustified terror which paralyzes needed efforts to convert retreat into advance."

"Ask not what your country can do for you—ask what you can do for your country."

"I know not what course others may take, but as for me, give me liberty or give me death."

It has been proven many times over that we are willing to die for America. Are we willing to live for her? It is imperative that we begin the moral revolution, and soon. I'm ready if you are. Will you join me?

"Our Father . . ."

Happy Birthday to America's Favorite Uncle

Dublin, Georgia
July 1, 1983

Mr. Samuel A. Merica
General Delivery
United States of America

Dear Uncle Sam:

The fact that I haven't been in contact with you for quite a while doesn't mean that I haven't been thinking about you. On the contrary, I think of you often and intend to write but just never seem to get around to it.

It seems that the older I get the more I think about and appreciate you. You have certainly been good to me down through the years and I really appreciate it. Actually, I feel somewhat guilty for not having been more attentive to your needs because you have really been attentive to mine.

I am prompted to write now because it dawned on me recently that you will be celebrating your 207th birthday on Monday, July 4. I just want to do more this year than pop an illegal firecracker and maybe mumble through half a verse of the "Star Spangled Banner."

You are my favorite uncle and I feel somewhat guilty about the manner in which I've treated you down through the years. I guess this is more of a confession than a letter, Uncle Sam.

Do you remember when you and I first got to know each other, on a first name basis? It was when you wrote me back in 1944. I was eighteen years old and had just finished Georgia Military College in Milledgeville. I remember well how you began the letter: "Greetings . . . you have been selected . . ."

Less than a month after receiving your letter, I boarded a bus and rode with about twenty-five others to Fort McPherson and was sworn into the United States Army. Eight weeks later I sailed on one of your naval ships, the U.S.S. *Storm King,* with 1799 others from Oakland, California to the Philippine Islands—with a brief stop at the small island of Eniwetok in the Marshall Islands.

I gave you two years in the army and then you brought me back home aboard the U.S.S. *West Point,* bought me a bus ticket from

San Francisco to San Antonio, and discharged me. You then gave me $300 mustering out pay and a train ticket to Georgia. But you weren't finished with me, Uncle Sam.

Once back home, you paid my way through two years of college at Georgia Southern and another at George Peabody College in Nashville and I left there with a Master of Arts degree and a teaching and coaching job at Dublin High School. I don't recall ever taking the time to write and say thank you, Uncle Sam. If it isn't too late, I'd like to do that now. After all, I gave you a mere two years and you reciprocated with three years of college and two degrees to help me make a living. That seems more than a fair deal for me, Uncle Sam.

Still, you weren't finished with me.

In 1964 you sent me yet another letter, to Wrightsville. And I remember well how you began that one, too: I am pleased to inform you that you have been appointed to the position of Special Agent of the Federal Bureau of Investigation. You should report for duty in Washington, D.C., on October 11 . . .

I reported as instructed, Uncle Sam, was sworn in, and trained for fourteen weeks at your Quantico Marine base in Virginia before reporting for my first assignment in Houston, Texas. During the next twenty years you sent me to Corpus Christi, Beaumont, Detroit, Marquette, Newark, New York, Las Vegas, and Savannah. In all these places you paid me well and permitted me to work with the finest people I've ever known, the men and women of the FBI. And, in 1965, when my mother and father became ill, you arranged for me to work in the Swainsboro FBI office so that I could be as near to them as possible, only thirty miles from their Lyons home. I won't ever forget that, Uncle Sam.

Then in 1974, after twenty years service in the FBI, you permitted me to retire and come to live in Dublin. You send me a nice check on the first of each month and will for as long as I live. And you also provide me with adequate health and life insurance.

Yes, sir, it seems that you have been mighty good to me, Uncle Sam.

Earlier in my letter, I mentioned that this is probably more of a confession than a letter. Well, the reason I said that is this: The more I dwell on the manner in which I've treated you the more I feel a sense of guilt. I have benefited from your efforts to make America a better place in which to live, Uncle Sam. I've ridden your roads, breathed your fresh air, played in your parks, and just generally enjoyed the good life. And yes, I've reaped the benefit of your schools.

On the other hand, I've acted somewhat in the manner of an ungrateful nephew. On many occasions I've been outspoken and critical of you and many of the people who represent you. I've hurled harsh and cutting remarks at senators and congressmen, but not once have I bothered to offer myself as a candidate for any public office. I have been content to sit back and criticize, but offered no solution to the situations about which I complained. In fact, and I am ashamed to confess this, there have been times when I didn't even bother to vote for or against those at whom I leveled the bulk of my criticism.

And once a year I mail in my income tax, but admittedly only after burning the midnight oil on the night of April 14 diligently searching for loopholes and exits to prevent paying it. And on April 15 I parade the streets brandishing a halo the size of a hula hoop and wearing a self-righteous grin as broad as a fourteen-foot double-wide.

It just seems to me that you have been a far better uncle than I have a nephew, Uncle Sam. And I would like to change that. I would like not to be so quick to criticize and condemn but rather to learn to exercise caution and patience before passing judgment on many of your proposals. I would like to arrive at the realization that you treat me better than any other uncle would in the entire world, and to appreciate that fully.

Basically, what I'm trying to say, Uncle Sam, is "thank you" for all you've done for me and I pray sincerely that I shall no longer take your deeds and concerns for granted. That's what I'd like to resolve as your 207th birthday approaches on Monday. You deserve so much more than I've given you.

Best wishes on your birthday.

Respectfully, your nephew,
Bo Whaley

One Right Was Left Out of the Constitution

I know it's pretty late in the game for me to be researching history. But I've been doing a little bit of that lately. What I have been researching is the Constitution of the United States—specifically the first ten amendments, commonly known as the Bill of Rights.

I know good and well I have rights, and my sole purpose in resorting to the Constitution is to try to find out what they are.

In reading the Bill of Rights, I determined that I have the right to: worship as I please—or not worship at all if I choose not to do so; keep and bear arms; not be quartered as a soldier in any house without the consent of the owner; be secure in my person, house, papers, and effects against unreasonable searches and seizures; not be compelled to incriminate myself in any criminal case; have a speedy and public trial by jury; not have excessive bail nor excessive fines imposed, as well as cruel and inhuman punishment; the guarantee that the enumeration in the Constitution of certain rights shall not be construed to deny or disparage others retained by the people; feel secure in the knowledge that powers not delegated to the United States by the Constitution, nor prohibited by it to the states, are reserved to the states respectively, or to the people.

Great! But that's as far as it went. I didn't find the right I was searching for: the right to a quiet and peaceful breakfast in any public restaurant.

I can't believe the framers of such a grand document as the Constitution could have overlooked such an important right, or else they were late sleepers and the kind who omitted breakfast. But if William Few and Abraham Baldwin, Georgia's signers of the Constitution, had been with me in Valdosta last Friday morning you can bet your grits that the right to a quiet and peaceful breakfast in any public restaurant would have been included.

Here's why:

After having spoken to the Valdosta Civitan Club on Thursday night, I retired to my room at the Ramada Inn. Very nice room, too. But then, motel rooms are somewhat like striptease dancers—you see one, you've seen 'em all. They vary very little, with some equipped a little more elaborately than others.

So when on the road and staying in a motel room, I look forward to a good, peaceful, and quiet breakfast—with a newspaper, plenty of time, and coffee. Some things in life just flat shouldn't be rushed. Breakfast is one.

The little cardboard sign on top of my motel room TV was encouraging: Enjoy a great breakfast, economically priced, with us. Two eggs, two pancakes, two strips of bacon, coffee and orange juice—$2.95. I decided I would do just that and went to sleep with visions of the economically priced breakfast dancing around in my little egg-shaped head.

I woke up bright and early Friday morning, and showered. I sang loud and good, like Bing Crosby, as I lathered, scrubbed, and thought about breakfast: "Oh, what a beautiful mooooorrrrrn-niinnng! Oh, what a beautiful day! I've got a wonderful feeeeellllliinnng! Everything's goin' my waaaaayyyyy!" (Boy, was I wrong! Had I only known what fate had in store for me in the restaurant I would have high-tailed it for the nearest Waffle House and a cup of coffee to go.)

Here's what happened.

I hadn't been seated more than two minutes when a man, his wife, and two boys (ages about five and three) came in and sat in the booth in front of mine. The boys were undoubtedly midget commandos on a secret mission for the Soviets with orders from the Kremlin to destroy all Ramada Inn restaurants. They almost completed their mission before my breakfast special arrived.

The first thing to go was the sugar. The three-year-old devoured five packages without bothering to open them. His brother chose to strew his allotment around, including my booth. Then, the three-year-old experienced the thrill of knowing just how much fun it was to tear up paper napkins while his brother played knock-down-the-catsup-bottle and turn-over-the-milk. I stared hard at both. The mother saw me and employed her best defensive weapon—a smile. Almost a misfire, but a smile nonetheless. Daddy? Hah! He could have cared less. He was nose-deep in his sports page. The two juvenile commandos could have unleashed a napalm attack and he'd have never known it.

I thought about what my friend and golf instructor, Joe Durant, said as we ate lunch one day and observed yet another search and destroy mission by a three-year-old in Dublin: "I'll tell you, that kid could could tear up an anvil with a feather."

Then came the kicker. Both boys armed themselves with knives

and forks. Me? Friend, I made it out of there. I know disaster in
the making when I see it.

The cashier made the usual inquiry as I paid my $2.95 plus tax,
"Did you enjoy your breakfast, sir?"

I borrowed a line from the late, great Groucho Marx. I had to,
the timing was perfect.

"I had a great breakfast—but this wasn't it."

Know ALL the words of "The Star Spangled Banner?"

Do you know all the words to "The Star Spangled Banner?" Do
you sing along with the celebrity who tests his hernia when he
reaches that part, "O'er the land of the free . . ." or do you munch
peanuts and hum or grunt an occasional word or phrase?

The next time you're out at the old ball park, just remember that
what you hear sung as "The Star Spangled Banner" is but the first
verse of what Sir Francis Scott Key wrote in 1814 just before dawn
after the British shelling of Fort McHenry, Md.

You might consider also that while Key wrote his famous song
in 1814, "The Star Spangled Banner" was not adopted officially
by Congress until 1931, 117 years after it was written and 88 years
after Key's death in 1843.

I found "The Star Spangled Banner" in its entirety a few weeks
ago. It hangs on a wall at the Dublin Elk's Lodge. I doubt that
there is a single person in Georgia who knows all the words.
Wanna' give it a try?

"The Star Spangled Banner"

"O', Say, can you see, by the dawn's early light.
What so proudly we hailed at the twilight's last gleaming
Whose broad stripes and bright stars through the perilous fight,
O'er the ramparts we watched were so gallantly streaming,
And the rocket's red glare, the bomb's bursting in air,
Gave proof through the night that our flag was still there.

O! Say, does that Star Spangled Banner still wave,
O'er the land of the free and the home of the brave.

On the shore, dimly seen through the mist of the deep,
Where the foe's haughty host in dead silence reposes,
What is that which the breeze, o'er the towering steep
As it fitfully blows, half conceals, half discloses.
Now it catches the gleam of the morning's first beam—
In full glory reflected, now shines on the stream;

'Tis the Star Spangled Banner, O! long may it wave
O'er the land of the free and the home of the brave.

And where is the band who so vauntingly swore
That the havoc of war and the battle's confusion
A home and a country would leave us no more?
Their blood was washed out their foul footstep's pollution.
No refuge could save the hierling and slave
From the terror of flight or the gloom of the grave!

And the Star Spangled Banner in triumph doth wave
O'er the land of the free, and the home of the brave

O! thus be it ever when freemen shall stand
Between their loved homes and the foe's desolation;
Bless'd with victory and peace, may our heaven-rescued land
Praise the power that hath made and preserved us a nation.
Then conquer we must, for our cause is Just—
And this be our motto—"In God is our trust!"
And the Star Spangled Banner in triumph shall wave
O'er the land of the free and the home of the brave."

—Francis Scott Key
September 14, 1814

Bo Whaley has won twenty-one awards as a columnist for the Dublin, Georgia, Courier Herald. He speaks to more than 200 audiences each year, hosts a morning radio talk show, "and loafs a lot."